TO

The alumni of Oral Roberts University

*Your work will exceed mine as you
listen to God's voice and obey Him*

Contents

The Truth about God's Voice
and His Messages

God's Messages to Me and
What They Mean to You

The
Ultimate
Voice

God's still small voice:
the clearest and loudest voice
you'll ever hear

Oral Roberts

Print ISBN 13: 978-1-50669-980-6
eBook ISBN 13: 978-1-50669-983-7

All Bible references are from the King James Version of the Holy Bible
unless otherwise specified.

Scripture quotations designated NKJV are from the New King James
Version. Copyright© 1979, 1980, 1982, Thomas Nelson, Inc., Publishers.

530 Great Road
Acton, MA 01720
800-562-2147
www.xanedu.com

God's Still Small Voice:
The Clearest and Loudest Voice
You'll Ever Hear

Growing up I never dreamed that God actually speaks to people today. If He was speaking to me during those early years, I certainly was not aware of it. Yet later in my life when I was aware He was speaking to me, *that I was actually hearing His voice*, I began a serious study of the Bible to try to understand these life-changing moments.

From my personal experience in hearing God's still small voice, I have come to know that the sound of His voice has cleared my mind of every other thought. The sound fills every fiber of my being so that I can detect nothing else. God's voice is the ULTIMATE VOICE rising within the human spirit.

Through more than sixty years as an author, educator, and evangelist, the most remarkable thing to me is that God has seen fit to speak to me in my spirit more than forty times.

I grew up the son of a farmer who later became a minister of the gospel. I loved him dearly. My father, Ellis Melvin Roberts, established twelve local churches in the area of Ada, Oklahoma,

where I was reared. My father never claimed that he heard God's voice, only that he felt His presence in his life and ministry.

Papa *impressed* me, but it was Momma who got *inside* me.

My mother, Claudius Priscilla Roberts, was of Cherokee Indian descent, only five feet tall. She was a quiet woman. She believed God speaks to everyone, although not in the same way. I never doubted she knew Him and He knew her, or that He spoke to her quite often. Many times I heard her talking to Jesus in the quiet of her labors as a housewife and mother. She talked to the Lord in the most natural way.

My talking, on the other hand, was quite unnatural. I grew up a stutterer. I couldn't imagine hearing God's voice when I couldn't even clearly hear my *own* words. My attempts to talk embarrassed me, sometimes to tears. Most of the time when I attempted to talk, the words would freeze in my throat. One year on the first day at school, the teacher asked each of us children to stand and give our names. Scared out of my wits, I stood and tried to say, "My name is Oral Roberts," but the words wouldn't come out and I fell back in my seat, crushed.

The kids laughed, then the teacher laughed. It drew me further inside myself. Anything the teacher asked me to do in writing I could do quite well, but trying to talk publicly tore me apart.

One day a group of school boys hemmed me up to get me to talk so they could hear my stammering and poke fun. I remember that I broke loose and ran home with them at my heels.

My mother heard them coming and met them at the gate and shamed them and sent them away. She led me into the house, and I sat down beside her and she said, "Oral, you were the last of my five children. Before you were born I asked God to give me a son with black hair and blue eyes who would be a preacher and carry His Word to the ends of the earth. Before you are grown, God will loose your tongue and you will talk just fine." I learned much later that my name, Oral, which my mother's niece gave me, means "spoken word."

Near my eighteenth birthday, a man of God prayed for me and I was healed, and since then I have fulfilled my mother's words to me; my life has been built around the spoken word.

I became a preacher and developed a large ministry, including forty years on national television, much of it in prime time. I carried God's healing power to my generation, built God a university, and now at ninety years old, I am still busy doing God's work.

My mother went home to be with God at age eighty-nine. Just before the end came she pulled my six-foot, one-inch frame down to her and told me, as she often did, "Oral, always stay little in your own eyes." Those are the last words I heard from her. They are very strong in me today as well as many of her other pearls: "Never strike back at your enemies. Leave them to God who says, 'Vengeance is Mine, I will repay,'" and "Keep your mind open to God for He will surely speak to you. You will hear His voice."

Just as I heard Momma's voice, I have heard God's voice, and you can too.

Sometimes I hear God's still small voice quite often. Other times it's been months, even a few years apart. I have sought never to be anxious, just to have a knowing inside me that God still speaks, in some way, to everyone on the planet. We only have to have a listening ear. As Jesus said, "If any man hear my voice, and open the door, I will come in to him, and will sup with him, and he with me" (REVELATION 3:20).

As you choose to read my book, I believe you may be quite surprised that more than once you have heard the STILL SMALL VOICE. Like me, at first, you may not have recognized that the Almighty would choose you as one of the *whosoever hears my voice.* Every person can hear—but he has to be listening. That's what my book is all about.

Nothing I have accomplished through the spoken word would have been possible except for this: I first heard the voice of God. Hearing from God has made all the difference in my life. I believe that can be true for your life, too, as you seek God's best and highest.

— ORAL ROBERTS

N o t e s

A Note to You, Reader, about the Way This Book Is Organized

There are two sections to this book.

The first section, which has four chapters, gives you what I understand in general terms about God's voice and the ways in which He speaks to human beings in today's world. You will find information about why I believe God speaks to every person, and what I believe God wants to convey to every person. You'll find my understanding about God's purposes for communicating with us. You'll also find my understanding about why some people don't seem to hear from God the way other people do, and you'll find information that I believe will be helpful to you as you evaluate whether you truly are hearing God's voice.

The information in the first chapters of this book is foundational. It is intended to give you a perspective about hearing God's voice as you read the later chapters.

The second section deals with some of the forty incidents in which I have heard God's voice. In each of these chapters, I relate one or more messages that God spoke to me. I tell what was happening in my life at the time I heard from God, and what happened in the aftermath as I attempted to obey what God had said to me. Then, I share with you how I believe the messages from God relate to you and may be an indicator of the way in which you might expect God to speak to you.

God doesn't change. The truth of God's words—whether spoken directly to your spirit, lived out in the ongoing life of Jesus, or written in the teachings of the Bible—does not change. God's truth is absolute and everlasting. The *applications* of God's words, however, change continually and they are unique to each person. I challenge you to look for the central truth of what God has said to me. That truth has relevance to you.

Perhaps most importantly, I challenge you repeatedly in this book to listen for God to speak. Expect Him to communicate with you. It is only as you hear from God that you truly can become all that God created you to be and do all that He purposes for you to accomplish in your lifetime.

The Truth about God's Voice and His Messages

CHAPTER ONE

Does God Speak to Every Person?

Yes.
And here's why I
believe that is true.

Behold, I stand at the door, and knock: if any man
hear my voice and open the door, I will come in to him,
and will sup with him, and he with me.
—REVELATION 3:20

For the past several years, I have had the privilege of meeting with small groups of twelve to twenty pastors and evangelists who have come to my home for an afternoon of conversation. These ministers have come for the primary purpose of asking me questions. I have simply made myself available to them, and they have taken advantage of the opportunity to discuss the things of God with me personally.

Some of those who have come have asked about healing and what it means to have a ministry of healing. Some have asked about the work of the Holy Spirit in a person's life. Some have asked how I built Oral Roberts University. Each group seems to have taken on a slightly different emphasis, depending on the men and women who gathered in my living room.

Nearly all of the groups, however, have had at least one person who was extremely interested in knowing,

"What does the voice of God sound like?"

Others in the group have usually picked up on that question, asking:

- How do you know it is God speaking?
- Does God speak to you all the time?
- How can I hear from God?
- Does God speak to every person?

On the one hand, I have been surprised at these questions, in part because I believe God speaks to every person who believes in Him, and even to some who don't. Yes, that includes *you.*

On the other hand, I have not been surprised, because in my experience, most people who *can* and *should* hear from God regularly, don't seem to. There seems to be a great deal of mystery about hearing from God, and some confusion about knowing whether the voice they are hearing inside them is God.

At the very core, however, I believe two things. First, every person *wants* to hear from God. And second, many people don't believe they are *worthy* to hear from God, and therefore, they are a little frightened to hear from God. After all, if and when God speaks to a person, there's only one response to be made: wholehearted obedience.

7 Reasons Why I Believe God Speaks to Every Person

There are at least seven reasons why I believe God speaks to every person, and especially to those who have received Jesus Christ as their Savior and have been filled with God's Holy Spirit.

1. It is the nature of God to communicate—to speak and to hear.

The Bible tells us that God created men and women in His own image—and part of God's image from the opening sentences of the Bible is to speak and in speaking, to create. The Word of God tells us that God *said*, and there was light...and then the light was divided from the darkness...and the firmament was established... and then the dry land...and then the grasses and trees and all manner of seed-bearing vegetation...and the sun, moon, and stars, and the fish and the fowl, and all living creatures. All were created by the spoken word of God.

God not only speaks, but God hears. The Bible reassures us repeatedly that when we call out to God, He hears us and responds to us.

2. We human beings have been created to communicate—to speak and to hear.

In creating mankind, God took the dust of the earth and fashioned it into a human being and then *breathed* His own spirit into man so that man became a living soul. He built into man the ability to give

names—which embodied the full identity and function—to all living creatures. And in the cool of the day, the Lord God walked with the man and woman He had placed in the Garden of Eden. God enjoyed fellowship with Adam and Eve and no doubt they talked over all of life as it unfolded before them. God answered their questions. He no doubt gave them daily guidance and they benefited greatly from the sheer comfort of His presence. I can almost hear Him laughing with them over the humorous things they must have experienced in any given day.

God created mankind for communication—with Himself, with other human beings, and as a means of taking dominion over the earth.

God built into mankind a desire for man to communicate with God. How do I know this? Because I have yet to meet a person who does not cry out to God in a time of tragedy or deep pain, or at a time of perilous danger or sickness that might lead to death. All of our deepest human cries—"Where are You, God?"... "Why me, God?"..."Are You real, God?"—presuppose the truth that God exists, God hears, and that man and God can and should communicate with each other!

I could write an entire book on the truths of the last few paragraphs, but let it suffice at this point to conclude: You were made to communicate with God and He desires to communicate with you. It is the way God created life to be on earth.

3. The Bible gives us a long history of recorded incidents in which God and man communicated very directly and specifically.

We find in the Bible evidence of short, long, and ongoing conversations that God had with such famous people as:

- Cain—God very directly spoke to Cain about his anger at having his offering refused, and then asked Cain about his brother Abel. (SEE GENESIS 4:2–16.)

- Noah—God gave Noah insider information about His plan to destroy the earth, and He gave specific instructions for building an ark and filling it with every sort of creature so that Noah and his family might escape a great flood. (SEE GENESIS 6:13–9:17.)

- Abram—God called Abram to go to a land that God would show him, and promised to make a great nation of him. (SEE GENESIS 12:1–2.) Through the years, God and Abram had repeated conversations about Abram's future, the change of Abram's name to Abraham, his wife Sarah, his sons Ishmael and Isaac, and the generations that were to follow Abraham in the land of Canaan.

- Isaac—God promised to bless Isaac if he would obey Him and stay in the land, sowing seed even in famine, and digging wells where there had been none before. (SEE GENESIS 26.)

- Jacob—God told Jacob where to build an altar to Him, and later changed Jacob's name to Israel. (SEE GENESIS 35.)

And so it goes, page after page, book after book—from the opening words of the Bible to the closing words.

God spoke to all of the great men and women of the Old Testament, including numerous conversations with Moses and later, his protégé Joshua. God spoke directly with all the great judges of Israel, including Gideon, Samson, Deborah, and others. He spoke to the great priests of Israel, including Samuel, who first heard God's voice as a child, and to the great kings including Saul, David, and Solomon. He spoke to all of the great prophets and through them, to the people of Israel. Many of the words of the Lord to these prophets became "books" of the Bible: Isaiah, Jeremiah, Ezekiel, Daniel, Hosea, Joel, Amos, Obadiah, Jonah, Micah, Nahum, Habakkuk, Zephaniah, Haggai, Zechariah, and Malachi.

God continued to speak throughout the New Testament, not only to and through Jesus Christ, God's only begotten Son, but also to Mary the mother of Jesus, Zacharias, John the Baptist, and the

apostles of Christ including Peter, James, John, and later, Paul. He spoke to countless leaders in the first-century church through men and women who "prophesied"—preaching, evangelizing, and teaching as the Holy Spirit compelled them to speak.

A person can hardly find any major incident in the Bible that does *not* include the phrase, "God said," or, "God spoke," or, "thus saith the Lord."

4. Jesus said so.

Jesus made several great statements about our communication with God the Father and with Himself, God's Son. Let me share just two of those with you.

On one occasion, Jesus encountered a man who had been born blind and He anointed his blind eyes with clay and spittle and then told him to go wash in the Pool of Siloam. The man did as Jesus said and immediately was able to see. Later, when he met Jesus face to face, Jesus asked him, "Do you believe on the Son of God?" The man said, "Lord, I believe." Jesus replied, "For judgment I am come into this world, that they which see not might see; and that they which see might be made blind." (SEE JOHN 9.) I relate strongly to this incident in Jesus' ministry. In many ways, I believe God has used me so that those who are sick might be healed, and those who have not heard God's voice might hear it. Not everybody who has heard my message has believed it or acted on it. Not everybody has been healed. But that was also true of Jesus: not everybody who heard Him believed in Him, acted on what He said, or followed Him.

Some religious leaders called Pharisees were standing nearby and they said to Jesus, "Are we blind also?" Jesus immediately began teaching, saying about Himself as the Great Shepherd, "He calleth his own sheep by name, and leadeth them out. And when he putteth forth his own sheep, he goeth before them, and the sheep follow him: for *they know his voice*. And a stranger will they not follow, but will flee from him: for *they know not the voice of strangers*" (JOHN 10:3–5, ITALICS ADDED FOR EMPHASIS).

As part of that teaching, Jesus also said, "I am the good shepherd, and know my sheep, and am known of mine" (JOHN 10:14). He also said these words that directly apply to those of us alive today: "And other sheep I have, which are not of this fold: them also I must bring, and *they shall hear my voice*; and there shall be one fold, and one shepherd" (JOHN 10:16, ITALICS ADDED FOR EMPHASIS).

Jesus *expected* His followers to hear Him—not only the Jews of His day, but people around the world in our day.

Later, as Jesus was standing before Pontius Pilate shortly before His death on the cross, Pilate asked Jesus if He was a king. Jesus said, "Thou sayest that I am a king. To this end was I born, and for this cause came I into the world, that I should bear witness unto the truth. *Every one that is of the truth heareth my voice*" (JOHN 18:37).

I have absolutely no doubt that any person who desires to hear and believe the TRUTH about God the Father, Jesus the Son, or the Holy Spirit will be given the truth, either directly or indirectly. God does not deny the heart's cry of any person in any culture on any continent who truly wants to know the TRUTH. He will speak to that person in a way that the person knows it is Him.

5. Jesus said the Holy Spirit would speak the truth of God to those who believe in Him.

Jesus told His followers that His Father would send the Holy Spirit to comfort and guide them after He had ascended to heaven: "I will pray the Father, and he shall give you another Comforter, that he may abide with you for ever; Even the Spirit of truth; whom the world cannot receive, because it seeth him not, neither knoweth him: but ye know him; for he dwelleth with you, and shall be in you" (JOHN 14:16–17).

As a normal function of His work, Jesus said, the Holy Spirit would speak TO and THROUGH those who believed in Him. On the

night before He was crucified, Jesus said, "I have yet many things to say unto you, but ye cannot bear them now. Howbeit when he, the Spirit of truth, is come, he will guide you into all truth: for he shall not speak of himself; but *whatsoever he shall hear, that shall he speak*: and he will shew you things to come" (JOHN 16:12–13, ITALICS ADDED FOR EMPHASIS).

Jesus stated that the Holy Spirit would bear witness of Him and lead His followers into all truth. The remainder of the New Testament writings makes it very clear that those who lived and ministered in the name of Jesus had no doubt about this as they taught, preached, and healed people in the decades that followed Jesus' death, resurrection, and ascension.

And...we should never forget that Jesus also spoke directly to Saul—whom we know as the apostle Paul—when Saul had not yet believed in Christ! As Saul traveled to Damascus with the intent of arresting Christians there, he encountered a brilliant light from heaven and fell to the earth, and the Bible says he "heard a voice saying unto him, Saul, Saul, why persecutest thou me? And he said, Who art thou, Lord? And the Lord said, I am Jesus whom thou persecutest" (ACTS 9:4–5).

Not only did Jesus speak directly to Saul—and in a way that seemed audible to Saul although to others around him the sound was like thunder—but the Lord also spoke to a disciple at Damascus named Ananias, saying to him in a vision, "Arise, and go into the street which is called Straight, and enquire in the house of Judas for one called Saul, of Tarsus: for, behold, he prayeth, And hath seen in a vision a man named Ananias coming in, and putting his hand on him, that he might receive his sight" (ACTS 9:11–12).

In just these few verses, we see that Jesus spoke—invisible to the natural eye and ear—directly to a zealous persecutor of the Christian faith, and then, in a vision to a Christian "layman" in Damascus, giving both Saul and Ananias a clear revelation of Himself and very direct instructions about what they were to do.

I am aware that there are those who believe the work of the Holy Spirit came to an end after the early church was established, but I am here to declare to you that I have found no evidence in the New Testament that the Holy Spirit has been withdrawn from the earth, that His work was ever redefined or diminished, or that He has a purpose in our lives different from His purpose in the lives of the first Christians. On the contrary, I see more evidence of the Holy Spirit speaking today than I have ever seen. His work is ongoing in ways too numerous and too great for us to grasp.

6. Momma and Papa told me so.

To some extent, we all are products of what we have been taught as children, and I have praised God more times than I can count that I grew up having the parents I had. I believe God used my parents to send me the message that God desires to have ongoing communication with every person.

Momma and Papa had a personal, direct, and intimate relationship with God. They talked to Him all the time. As a boy, I took great comfort when I'd lie in bed at night and hear them call my name, and the names of my brothers and sister, to the Lord.

Once when I was a young boy, I awoke early one morning and heard my parents talking to Jesus: "Jesus, we love You. Jesus, remember us and our family, and all those we are praying for. Remember Vaden and Oral, that they will know You and Your plan for their lives and follow it."

Before I realized what I was doing, I punched my older brother Vaden, who was asleep nearby, and said, "Vaden, Jesus is in our house!"

"No, He's not," Vaden said, and promptly went back to sleep. Vaden was very sleepy-headed, but I awakened at the smallest sound. I punched him again and said, "Yes, He is! Papa and Momma are talking to Him. Don't you hear them?"

Eventually of course, I learned Jesus was not there in the flesh in our house, but as far as my parents were concerned, He was

present in the fullness of His reality. They definitely were on speaking terms with Him.

I also discovered through the years that everything Momma and Papa taught me about Jesus, and everything they told me God had said to them about me, came to pass. As two of the people I have trusted most in my life, Momma and Papa never gave me any reason to doubt that God speaks to human beings.

7. I have heard God speak.

I have heard God speak to me more than forty times in my life—as of this writing. I am still open to hearing from Him again! His words to me have been life-changing every time. God's words have given me comfort and direction and filled me anew with His powerful presence. In the chapters that follow, I will be sharing a number of those messages from God with you.

Can I fully explain how I hear and how I know it is God? No. As is true with many aspects of God's nature, hearing from infinite and almighty God is not something that can be fully grasped or understood by any finite mind, no matter how spiritual a person may be. But, I can grasp and understand *partially* what it means to hear from God. And in the following pages I will share with you what I know to be true about God's communication with us.

Am I sure that I heard from God? Absolutely. As I have said through the years, I know that I know that I know. There is no doubt in me that I have heard, in part because of the way in which I heard, what I heard, and most of all, what happened when I acted in obedience on what I heard.

A man once said to a little boy, "You claim eating several unripe green apples can make a person sick. On what basis do you make that claim?"

The little boy pointed to a small pile of apple cores, rubbed his stomach, and said in a puny voice, "I have inside information."

I not only have "inside information" that God has spoken to me, but I also have "outside evidence."

Inside Information Must Produce Outside Evidence

Jesus once said to His followers, "The words that I speak unto you I speak not of myself: but the Father that dwelleth in me, he doeth the works. Believe me that I am in the Father, and the Father in me: or else believe me for the very works' sake" (JOHN 14:10–11).

If you want to know if I heard from God, my first response is to say, "Judge for yourself. Take a look at what happened when I acted on what God said to me." I am very happy to let my deeds speak for themselves, and especially so if a person truly will take a look at my deeds without any preconceived opinions about me personally.

Did God tell me to have a healing ministry? Yes. I can point to decades of experience and countless people who were healed in the healing services I have conducted through the years.

Did God tell me to build Him a university? Yes. I can show you the beautiful campus on rolling hills along South Lewis Avenue in Tulsa, Oklahoma, and I can tell you stories of thousands of alumni who are circling the world, serving others with excellence and with the healing power of God flowing through their lives.

Did God tell me to go on television to preach the gospel and pray for the sick? Yes. I can point to hundreds of thousands of people through the years who have written letters to tell me that they either came to know Jesus as their Savior, they were healed, or they were helped in practical areas of their lives in some way because they heard me preach and pray on television.

God not only confirms His words to a person's heart, but He confirms His words in the reality of *results*.

I caution any person to evaluate the advice or claims that another person may make, saying, "God told me." Check out the results. Take a look at the person's track record. I gladly offer you mine to examine.

The Bible tells us that God's Word is always fruitful. One of my favorite passages in the Old Testament is this:

> For as the heavens are higher than the earth, so are my ways higher than your ways, and my thoughts than your thoughts.
>
> For as the rain cometh down, and the snow from heaven, and returneth not thither, but watereth the earth, and maketh it bring forth and bud, that it may give seed to the sower, and bread to the eater:
>
> So shall my word be that goeth forth out of my mouth: *it shall not return unto me void, but it shall accomplish that which I please, and it shall prosper in the thing whereto I sent it* (ISAIAH 55:9–11, ITALICS ADDED FOR EMPHASIS).

God doesn't speak just to hear Himself talk. He speaks to make real things happen in a real world.

CHAPTER TWO

Why Doesn't Every Person Hear God's Voice?

Evaluate your willingness to hear.

[Jesus said,] He that hath ears to hear,
let him hear.
—MATTHEW 11:15

When I tell people that I believe God speaks to every person, some look away and say softly and almost wistfully, "I've never heard Him speak to me." Others have asked me very directly, "If God wants to speak to every person, why haven't I heard from Him?"

I believe there are four main reasons why a person doesn't hear God's voice. Any one of these reasons can function as an earplug in the spirit of a man or woman.

I find the words that God spoke to the prophet Ezekiel somewhat amusing. God told Ezekiel that the people couldn't see and hear because they were rebellious. And then He said, "Prepare thee stuff for removing" (EZEKIEL 12:3).

If you aren't hearing God's voice clearly in your spirit, you may need to do some "removing" of whatever obstacle is in the way.

Reason #1:
Some People Are
Afraid to Hear

The Bible makes it very clear that Adam and Eve had a walking-and-talking relationship with God. After Adam and Eve disobeyed God and ate fruit from the forbidden Tree of the Knowledge of Good and Evil, they sought to hide themselves from God's presence. God saw them, of course, but He called to them with a question: "Where are you?" (GENESIS 3:9, PARAPHRASED). I believe God asks every person that question today if that person is running from God, hoping that God will not discover him in his sin and rebellion. The question is not one of mere "location"—God knew Adam and Eve were hiding among the trees of the garden. God was asking them, "Where are you in your relationship with Me?" That's the key question every human being must answer.

Adam said, "I heard thy voice in the garden, and I was afraid, because I was naked; and I hid myself" (GENESIS 3:10). Adam knew that he had disobeyed God and was subject to consequences for his rebellion. He was *afraid*. He felt utterly exposed before God and no doubt was trembling in his fear.

I routinely meet people who are afraid of God. They regard Him as a mean judge who is just waiting to jump up from His throne in heaven, pounce on them in a swirl of vengeance, and punish them severely and perhaps fling them into hell in a furious rage.

Some of the fear people feel is because they have sinned and they know it. Even intuitively and subconsciously, they know that sin results in separation from God. I have good news for you if you are a person who fears God because of sin. God says you can confess that you are a sinner, ask Him to forgive you, and He will! There is a very simple solution for the sin problem in your life. Admit your sin to God and receive His forgiveness. There's nothing long and involved about believing in Jesus as God's Son and receiving the forgiveness Jesus made possible through His death on the cross. A simple but sincere statement is all that is required: "Lord, I'm a sinner. I accept what Jesus did on my behalf. Please forgive me and put me in right relationship with You."

Some people have false guilt. They have been caught up in the sinful behavior of other people and they have laid claim to sins that aren't their own. Still other people don't believe God will forgive them because they have sinned too greatly or too often.

Hear the good news of the Bible, which says, "If we confess our sins, he is faithful and just to forgive us our sins, and to cleanse us from all unrighteousness" (1 JOHN 1:9).

If fear is keeping you from hearing God's voice, ask yourself if that fear is related to your understanding of sin and its consequences. Deal with the sin issue.

Don't let sin, guilt, or false guilt keep you from hearing God.

Reason #2: Some People Feel Unworthy to Hear

A second reason that people don't hear God's voice is that they feel totally unworthy to hear.

I've learned a lot about self-value and worthiness through the years. It seems abundantly clear to me that *people* make people feel unworthy. God never says to a person, "You are unworthy of Me."

I grew up in a preacher's home, and there were a number of people in my father's church who seemed to adopt the stance, "We'll keep Brother Roberts humble by keeping him poor." They somehow thought enforced poverty resulted in humility and that humility automatically led to greater spirituality. From my experience, poverty only made us hungry and barefoot. That kind of poverty-produces-spirituality thinking has nothing to do with anything Jesus taught or modeled in His life. I have never seen a person come closer to God through the method of poverty.

Through the years I have encountered people who made other kinds of false connections and drew other kinds of false conclusions. As examples: a person needs to remain uneducated in order to be totally open to what God says to their spirit...a preacher needs to go into a pulpit without much advance preparation in order to receive a genuine "anointing" on the delivery of his sermon...or a person needs to suffer in patience and silence until God takes pity.

The root of all these lines of reasoning is this: A person must show himself worthy—through self-effacing and self-debasing actions—before God will speak to that person, save him, heal him, use him, or send him a miracle.

I have spent nearly seventy years speaking against that kind of "stinkin' thinkin'."

Still others are victims of bad teaching. They have listened to so-called "ministers" hammer falsehoods into their skulls. As examples:

- "You are unqualified to experience God's presence directly—you need me to be your intermediary." Not so!

- "You cannot understand God's Word or interpret it accurately, so you shouldn't read His Word for yourself— you need me to interpret the Bible for you." Not true!

- "You are too corrupt or too vile in your humanity to even approach a holy God—you need to trust me to deal with God on your behalf." No!

Nothing could be further from God's truth than those three statements.

Our worthiness before God has nothing to do with what we do or don't do in our natural abilities, apart from believing in Jesus. We are not made worthy by our actions or our attitudes. We are made worthy totally by the actions of Christ Jesus and our acceptance of Him. It is God who says we are worthy of His salvation, His free gift of eternal life, His blessings, and His presence.

How dare we say we are poor in any area of our life when God calls us to be prosperous and successful in every area of our life!

How dare we say that we are worms and of no account when God calls us His beloved children, His mighty men of valor on this earth, His witnesses, and His ambassadors!

How dare we say we are unlovable or unworthy of God's presence when God calls out to us, saying, "You are forgiven, you are loved, you are healed, you are delivered from evil, you are My chosen child!"

If feelings of unworthiness are keeping you from hearing God's voice, face up to the truth about yourself—hear the truth of GOD in His Word, not the lies errant men speak to you from their own self-centered desires for power or financial gain. If you have believed

in Jesus as your Savior, you are worthy. God says so. Agree with Him.

The Bible tells us to "lift up our heads" in expectancy and excitement before God. In other words, take heart! God has something to say to you. Set yourself to hear it.

Reason #3:
Some People Decide
They Don't WANT to Hear

The third reason many people don't hear God's voice is they simply have determined IN ADVANCE that they don't *want to do,* and therefore, *will not do* anything God might tell them to do. They don't want to hear anything that God might say because they don't want to change their ideas, their attitudes, or their behavior in any way.

Such a person has closed his mind and heart to God. The Bible word for that is "rebellion." The rebellious person does not hear because he simply does not **want** to hear.

Rebellion, in its simplest form, is putting one's self in opposition to God.

God told this to the prophet Ezekiel: "Thou dwellest in the midst of a rebellious house, which have eyes to see, and see not; they have ears to hear, and hear not: for they are a rebellious house" (EZEKIEL 12:2).

Rebellious people often try to justify their rebellion by citing something they believe God has done or that God is by nature.

Years ago, I encountered a man who blamed God for every bad thing that had ever happened to him or to those he loved. He gave me a long laundry list of bad things that had happened in his life, and he concluded, "If God is like that, I want nothing to do with Him."

I said to him, "You say, 'If God is like that.' The truth is, God isn't like that. God did not send these negative things into your life. You have confused the work of God and the work of the devil." Jesus said that it is the devil who comes to steal from us, destroy us, and kill us. Jesus made it clear that He came to give us both eternal life, and an abundant life on this earth. (SEE JOHN 3:16 AND JOHN 10:10.)

For nearly seventy years, I have preached a very simple truth about God: God is a *good* God. The corollary truth is this: The devil is a decidedly *bad* devil.

Jesus came to seek out and rescue those who are lost—which means "out of relationship with God." Jesus gave His life as a sacrifice so that mankind could be restored to God fully. Then, Jesus sent the Holy Spirit so mankind might walk in daily obedience and be in daily communication with God the Father. God is loving, merciful, longsuffering, and gracious. He gives good things to His children. He does not seek to curse you, but to bless you. Those who stand in rebellion before God hurt only themselves by not availing themselves of a good and loving God's help.

Jesus said to His followers, "If ye then...know how to give good gifts unto your children, how much more shall your Father which is in heaven give good things to them that ask him?" (MATTHEW 7:11).

Rebellion isn't limited to blaming God. There are some people who draw a prior conclusion that if God speaks to them, God is going to ask them to go someplace they don't want to go, do something they don't want to do, or engage in an experience that they don't want. They see the commands of God as being too difficult, too demanding, or too restrictive. And therefore, they turn a deaf ear toward God.

In truth, God asks us to do the very things in life that He pre-designed us and equipped us to do. He asks us to do things that are in keeping with the basic talents, abilities, desires, and dreams that He placed within us. He asks us to go places that will provide opportunities for our maximum fulfillment. He asks us to accomplish things that give meaning and purpose to life. He leads us into relationships with people who can help us, encourage us, bless us, and love us.

The commandments of God were not given to restrict man from things that are pleasurable or fulfilling. They were given so that man might have the maximum opportunity to experience happiness and fulfillment!

God doesn't want people to live in misery—rather, He wants our lives and our joy to be *full*. He wants every one of His children to live in wholeness and to have a tremendous sense of hope.

If you are refusing to hear God's voice because you are anticipating that you won't *like* what God has to say…consider the very real possibility that you are missing out on the greatest adventure of your life. I believe that what God has to say to you just may be the most exciting thing you ever hear!

Reason #4: Some People Don't Believe God Exists…or that He Speaks

Fourth and finally, there are some people who do not hear from God because they do not believe God exists, or that God speaks.

The Bible tells us, "Without faith it is impossible to please him: for he that cometh to God must believe that he is, and that he is a rewarder of them that diligently seek him" (HEBREWS 11:6).

God has given to you and to every other person an ability to *believe*. (SEE ROMANS 12:3.) You have been given the privilege by God of choosing in what you will believe, in whom you will believe, and the degree to which you will believe. Those are aspects of free will He has given to every person.

If you do not believe in God…chances are you will not say anything to Him and therefore, you aren't likely to hear anything back from Him.

If you do not believe that God will answer you when you ask something of Him...chances are that you don't hear His answers.

On the other hand, if you believe in God and believe that He desires to communicate with you, you are likely to hear from God in profound ways.

Are You Really Willing to Listen?

The ultimate question a person must ask of himself when it comes to hearing God's voice is this:

Do you really want to hear?

Do you have a burning desire to hear from God?

Are you at a point in your life where you believe that you *must* hear from God—that your very life and future depend on it?

Are you so in need of hearing from God that you will not speak or act until He tells you what to do?

I've been there. I know how you feel.

While we cannot force God to speak to us on our terms or when we want Him to speak, we can have what the Bible calls a "heart" for God. We can have a hunger to hear from God and to know what He wants for us, from us, and desires to do through us.

The Bible tells the story of a king in Israel's history who faced impossible military odds. Three mighty armies were converging upon Jerusalem. This king, named Jehoshaphat, went to the outer courts of the great temple in Jerusalem and cried out to God, "We have no might against this great company that cometh against us; neither know we what to do: but our eyes are upon thee."

The Bible then says that "all Judah stood before the LORD, with their little ones, their wives, and their children." In other words,

they stood in God's presence and waited for what God would say. (SEE 2 CHRONICLES 20:12–13.)

If you truly want to hear from God, turn toward Him. Express your deep desire to hear from Him. Ask Him to open your ears to hear, your eyes to see, and your mind to take in *everything* He might want to say to you.

And if you think you hear His voice begin to speak inside you, stand still and listen. Don't act too quickly. Don't dismiss what you are hearing.

A young lad named Samuel became a helper to an old high priest named Eli. Young Samuel heard a voice calling his name and he went running to Eli, thinking Eli was calling for him. Eli hadn't said a word. This happened again...and then again. Finally Eli realized that it was God who was attempting to speak to the lad. Eli said to Samuel, "It shall be, if he call thee, that thou shalt say, Speak, LORD, for thy servant heareth" (1 SAMUEL 3:9).

Make that your posture before God.

Prepare your heart to listen.

CHAPTER THREE

God Is the Supreme Communicator

God has something purposeful to say and an effective way of saying it.

[The Lord said,] With him [Moses] will I speak mouth to mouth, even apparently, and not in dark speeches, and the similitude of the Lord shall he behold.

—Numbers 12:8

A number of years ago I had a conversation with one of our professors at Oral Roberts University. We were discussing the topic of communication—and more specifically, what made communication effective.

This professor said, "From my years of study in this area, I have come to agree with other communication researchers that there are four basic facets of communication: the speaker, the message, the delivery method or channel of communication, and the hearer. That last element is the most problematic. No matter who the speaker may be, and no matter how important the message or technologically advanced the method of delivery, if the hearer isn't hearing, there is no communication."

"What can a speaker do in such cases?" I asked.

"A speaker can just keep trying, saying his message in as many ways as possible through as many delivery methods as possible."

That's the way God communicates with us.

He speaks to each of us a message that reflects both His eternal and His "today" plans and purposes. He speaks to us in an infinite variety of ways. He longs for us to hear and to that end, He keeps speaking even when we choose not to hear Him or seem incapable of discerning His voice.

If we truly are going to hear from God and get His message straight, we must choose to hear, and part of our hearing is going to involve having a good understanding of the One who is speaking. We must openly acknowledge several great truths about God, the Speaker.

God Has a Reason for Speaking

Everything God has ever done, is doing, or will ever do is "on purpose." God acts with intention and according to a sovereign plan and design of His own creation.

God made you for a purpose. He designed you in a unique way to fulfill that purpose. It is a purpose that fits into His overall plan for all mankind through the ages and into eternity.

We say about God that God is "omnipresent." He is always present—in every moment we know as time but beyond time, throughout all eternity. He has always been and will always be.

What does this mean to us when it comes to hearing God's voice?

It means first and foremost that God speaks to His children from a perspective of eternity. God wants our eternal good and He is working all things according to His plan for our eternal benefit. (SEE ROMANS 8:28.) We may fail at a particular task or project, but God does not fail. He takes what we do and weaves it into His eternal plan in such a way that our efforts accomplish His purposes, even if we fall short of man's approval, applause, or appreciation.

God will not say anything to us that is contrary to His total plan for the redemption of mankind and the establishment of His kingdom.

In a very practical way, God will not say anything to a particular individual that is not in full alignment with the overall truths of the Bible. God does not contradict Himself.

Neither will God say anything to a particular individual that causes harm to the body of Christ. God always moves to build up, encourage, and bless His people *as a whole.*

And, God will not say anything to a particular individual that causes a person to do harm to himself. Just as God desires for the body of Christ to work in harmony and as a whole, so God desires for every individual to be made well in spirit, mind, body, and relationships, and to function as a *whole* human being.

God always speaks from the backdrop of eternal truth and eternal purpose.

A NOW Word for Today's Need.

Just as God is the governor of ALL time and eternity, so God is the God of every second of time as we know it. God enters into

each moment of a human being's life. God speaks in the NOW of life.

A number of years ago I met with two Jewish rabbis about a particular matter that I believed was of mutual interest to us. I recently met with one of my former associates at Oral Roberts University, who was present at the meeting and recalled it vividly. He said, "I remember that you opened the meeting by asking, 'Does God still speak to people today?' The silence in the room was so thick you could have cut it with a knife. The rabbis knew that your opening statement went to the very heart of the matter. If they said 'yes,' then they had to admit there was at least a possibility that you had heard from God on the matter we were about to discuss. If they said 'no,' they had to defend their position theologically and biblically, and they knew they were at odds with each other in what they believed about God's working in today's world."

This colleague reminded me of a central truth to hearing God's voice: It isn't enough to believe that God *has spoken*. Part of believing that God exists and that God speaks is believing that God speaks *today*. He speaks in the NOW of every circumstance, situation, and relationship. He has a NOW answer for every current question. He has a NOW solution for every current problem. He has a NOW word for every current emotion, opinion, or attitude.

God does not change. He is the same yesterday, today, tomorrow, and forever. He is not swayed from His eternal plans and purposes. If God has ever spoken, He speaks NOW.

He has a NOW word for the exact need you are facing...now.

God Has Unlimited Ways and Means

We must never lose sight of the truth that God is God. God does what God wants to do, when He wants to act, and for the purposes that are of His choosing. God chooses or creates His own methods, very often creating new methods for specific times and situations. God is never bound by methodology or natural law.

I have read the Bible from cover to cover more times than I can recall and I have noticed this: God only called upon one person and his family to build one ark as a means of escape from one worldwide flood. God only parted the Red Sea once and gave to only one man one miracle-producing rod. God only called upon one man to use one slingshot and one smooth round stone on one occasion to kill one enemy of His people. God only made a rustling sound of thousands of hoofbeats in the tops of the trees in one grove to scare away one threatening enemy on one occasion. God only caused the sun to stand still on one occasion.

I could give you numerous other examples from the Bible and from history. Time and time again, God has used and continues to use distinctive methods that are beyond mankind's imagination, to accomplish distinctive results that are rooted in very specific situations in very specific locations at very specific times.

Absolute PRINCIPLES but an Infinite Variety of METHODS.

As absolute as God's PRINCIPLES are, so God's METHODS are just that varied and unique.

Principles do not change.

Methods do.

God will not speak anything to your spirit that violates any unchanging absolute command or principles stated in His Word, but He may tell you to take on a task in a way that has never been tried before. He may ask you to invent a new technology, try a new approach, frame the truth of your message to the world in new terminology, or use a delivery system that has never before been seen on this earth.

God has never stopped creating. He has never stopped designing. He has never stopped putting into place new systems, new uses, and new protocols for chemicals, creatures, and natural laws that have been in existence from the beginning of the world as we know it. God has never stopped pouring out His ideas from the windows of heaven into the hearts and minds of people who will translate those ideas into a new product, a new approach, or a new insight into God's nature.

When it comes to the way God communicates with us, His methods are infinite. Even so, the foremost ones we find in the Bible seem to be these:

- **God speaks through His prophets and fellow saints—** who are chosen by God to speak a specific word as they are empowered by the Spirit to do so.

- **God speaks through His written Word**. At times, words or phrases from God's Word seem to leap from the pages of the Bible to capture our thoughts and touch our hearts in inescapable and life-changing ways.

- **God speaks through signs and wonders**, always pointing us toward the power of Jesus to save, heal, and deliver mankind.

- **God speaks through the glories of the natural world**. The heavens and the earth both are filled with declarations of His power and glory that compel us to give all praise to God the Father.

- **God speaks through visions and dreams**, very often giving highly specific information about what to do, when to act, what to say, and where to go.

- **God speaks through angels**, who come as messengers sent by heaven to help us, guard us, and inform us.

- **God speaks through impressions and images that become engraved on human hearts and minds** so that we cannot forget who God is and what He desires for us.

- **And, He speaks to us in words** that fully occupy all of our being so that there seems to be no voice and no sound other than the Voice speaking within us.

I have heard God speak to me in each of these ways. You may have heard Him in these ways, too, or at least in a few of these ways. I make no claim that these are *all* of the ways God speaks to an individual, but I do make a claim that we each need to be open to *all* of the ways God might choose to speak to us.

I have encountered Christians—even very devout men and women—who have told me very openly and candidly that they believe God only speaks through His written Word. They believe everything a person ever needs to hear from God can be heard through the silent mental process of reading words on a page.

My response is a question to them: "Is that the only way God speaks...or is that the only way you are willing to hear Him?"

A number of years ago when the telegraph was the latest marvel in communications technology, a new telegraph office opened and advertisements were posted throughout the community for a person to become the local telegraph operator. The waiting room outside the room where the telegraph equipment was located was soon filled with young men applying for the job.

One man walked into the room, and after just a few moments, walked boldly to the door of the interview room, opened it, and walked in. He came out a few minutes later and announced to all of the other young men in the waiting room, "You can go home. I got the job."

The other young men were angry. "What gave you the right to barge into the interview room like that? Why weren't we given an opportunity to interview for the job?"

The man asked for silence, and in the silence, a series of tapping sounds could be heard faintly. The young man said, "Do you hear that sound? It is a telegraph machine using dots and dashes to say, 'If you can understand this message, come through the door on the other side of the waiting room.' I got the job because I understood what the dots and dashes were saying."

If you choose to limit God to using only your chosen method of communication, you may just miss out on the most amazing opportunity you will ever have for the most fulfilling life imaginable.

Listen.

And then, listen more closely.

Listen more intently.

Listen with a truly open heart.

God Speaks in Your Inner Man

Every person has been given a spirit that is capable of experiencing God. Every person has an inner ability to see and hear.

We are just now beginning to explore more fully these concepts of Inner Vision and Inner Hearing. I believe much more will be understood about both of these spiritual abilities in the coming months and years. What I do know is this:

- Our Inner Vision and Inner Hearing are for the purpose of communicating with God.

- Inner Vision and Inner Hearing are CAPACITIES that have been created within us so that God might communicate with us.

A few people are already speaking and writing about a person's "inner voice" or "inner sight." They seem to be referring to a person's deepest intuitions and subconscious understanding. They are referring to a person giving expression to his or her deepest dreams and desires.

I am referring to something much different. True Inner Vision is not something you drum up, concoct, or do according to your own abilities, desires, or sensitivities. True Inner Hearing is not something that reflects your deepest ideas, attitudes, or feelings. True Inner Vision and true Inner Hearing are CAPACITIES. They are somewhat like vacuums or containers within us for GOD to show us what HE wants us to see, and for us to hear what HE wants us to hear.

The Bible tells us about a dramatic incident in the life of the prophet Elijah. At the time of this incident, Israel was suffering from a great drought that had lasted three years. The people were suffering and were desperate for rain. Elijah was led by God to use the drought as a sign to God's people that God alone is sovereign over all things.

Elijah called the false prophets of Baal to a showdown encounter on top of Mount Carmel. The prophets of Baal built an altar and slaughtered animals and placed them on the altar. Then they cut themselves with knives and leaped about the altar for hours, crying out to Baal to send down fire to consume and thus "accept" their sacrifice. Nothing happened.

Elijah then built an altar and prepared animals for sacrifice, made a trench around the altar, and filled the trench with water. For good measure, he also thoroughly doused the wood under the sacrifice, the altar, and the animals with water. Then he prayed a simple prayer: "Hear me, O LORD, hear me, that this people may know that thou art the LORD God, and that thou hast turned their heart back again." Immediately fire fell upon the altar, totally consuming the sacrifice, the wood, the stones of the altar, the water in the trench, and even the dust around the altar!

In the wake of this display of God's awesome power, Elijah was empowered by God to kill the prophets of Baal, and then to send word to King Ahab that it was about to rain! (SEE 1 KINGS 18.)

Ahab's queen, a wicked woman named Jezebel, was furious that her prophets to Baal had been killed. She issued a death sentence on Elijah and Elijah ran for his life, traveling ultimately to a distant cave on Mount Horeb far to the south of Mount Carmel. There, the Lord spoke to him, asking, "What doest thou here, Elijah?"

God certainly knew where Elijah was, and why Elijah was in the cave. The fact was, God had not commanded Elijah to flee, nor had

God directed him to go to Mount Horeb. God was asking Elijah, in effect, "Why are you here in a place I did not send you?"

Elijah told the Lord about his troubles and conveyed to the Lord his belief that he was the only true prophet of God left in all Israel. God called Elijah to a meeting. He said, "Go forth, and stand upon the mount before the LORD."

Elijah did as he was commanded and we read this account of what happened:

> Behold, the LORD passed by, and a great and strong wind rent the mountains, and brake in pieces the rocks before the LORD; but the LORD was not in the wind: and after the wind an earthquake; but the LORD was not in the earthquake:
>
> And after the earthquake a fire; but the LORD was not in the fire: and after the fire a still small voice.
>
> And it was so, when Elijah heard it, that he wrapped his face in his mantle, and went out, and stood in the entering in of the cave. And, behold, there came a voice unto him (1 KINGS 19:11–13).

I see no evidence in the Word of God that God speaks to us by means of circumstances or situations. He does not speak to us through natural disasters or catastrophic calamities. As fierce and powerful as the wind, earthquake, and fire may have been in Elijah's experience on Mount Horeb, there was no message from God in those natural events other than the truth that they were *not* message-bearing natural phenomena.

God speaks to us in our inner being. Even when He speaks to us in the wide variety of ways I mentioned earlier in this chapter, the *message* from God comes to us *on the inside of us.*

- It is in our inner man that we interpret the words of God's prophets and His angelic messengers, and make decisions in response to those words.

- It is in our inner man that we are convicted by God's Word, draw meaning from it, and feel instructed by it.

- It is in our inner man that we see miraculous signs and wonders as pointing toward Jesus.

- It is in our inner man that we interpret the glories of nature as examples of God's infinite and creative power and authority over all the material realm.

- It is in our inner man that we experience visions and dreams, and have meaning for them upon awaking.

- It is in our inner man that God speaks by His Spirit.

People have asked me repeatedly, "Do you hear an *audible* voice?"

My response is this: "On those occasions when God has spoken to me in words and sentences, I have heard God's message filling me completely on the inside in such a way that I can't hear and am not aware of anything else on the outside."

The voice is not from the outside. It is on the inside.

The voice is compelling and penetrating.

Is it a "still voice"? Yes, in the sense that everything around me becomes exceedingly still. Few of us ever hear anything in this life against a background of *total* silence. When God speaks into our Inner Hearing it is as if He is speaking into a vacuum of absolute silence. His voice is an extension of the stillness and is inseparable from the stillness. His words are like the calm eye in all of life's storms.

Is it a "small voice"? Yes, in the sense that God doesn't shout. He speaks and He commands, but He doesn't yell. He doesn't have to. When everything else is silent—as if all the world has stopped, and time and space are of no concern— God's voice becomes very plain. His voice is intimate in tone. It is measured but not slow. It is exact but not pedantic. It is the sound of love that has taken on the form of language.

I hear God inside my total being and His words address my total being. His words consume my thoughts, my attitudes, and my entire body. His words are attention-demanding and simultaneously

compelling, challenging, and commanding. They require that I respond *with all my being*.

When I read the Bible account of what happened to Elijah on Mount Horeb, I find myself saying with everything within me, "Yes! That's the way it is!" God speaks to the inner person, and in doing so, the same Voice that commanded the earth to rise from the waters... the sun, moon, and stars to take their places in the heavens; and the forces of life to spring forth on this earth—that same Voice fills us as God's finite vessels made of clay so that something new is created in us...and it is for our good and for the good of mankind.

In listening for God's voice, we are wise to get our eyes OFF the world around us. We are wise to shut down the noise that most of us surround ourselves with during every waking hour. We are wise to take control of all our anxious thoughts and worries and fears so that we truly think of NOTHING except God's vast love for us and His wisdom in all things, power over all things, and presence at all times. We are wise to go in silence before the Lord and LISTEN.

Then, listen even more intently.

Listen day by day.

And, listen until our hearts melt before Him and our minds are willing to hear *anything* He might say to us.

The Nature of God's Messages

God's words are forever... and for today.

Behold, a bright cloud overshadowed them: and behold
a voice out of the cloud, which said, This is my beloved
Son, in whom I am well pleased; hear ye him.

—MATTHEW 17:5

As I have read and studied the Bible through the years, as well as several hundreds of books that might be categorized as historical accounts or biographies, I have come to a conclusion: When God gets ready to change a nation, to lift an empire, or to bring forth deliverance to man, He has a baby born.

A person once said, "Every new birth is God's way of confirming that life should go on." When God gets ready to do ANYTHING new on the earth, He causes a baby to be born. God changes history through great individuals. God influences nations through great individuals. God brings about great spiritual revivals, new waves of thinking, and new systems for spreading His truth...through great individuals.

When God was ready to establish a people for Himself, He caused Abraham to be born.

When God was ready to free His people from Egyptian bondage, He caused Moses to be born.

When God was ready for a new shift in the priesthood and the inauguration of kings in Israel, He caused Samuel to be born.

When God was ready for mankind to be redeemed fully, He caused Jesus to be born.

Every child is birthed in God's "fullness of time." God creates every child for a specific time and with a specific purpose to impact his generation in a godly way. We each are created for service—to be of use to others. We are created to fulfill a specific role in God's redemptive plan for all mankind.

But how do we come to know our purpose and what it is that God regards as our destiny in life?

God tells us.

He speaks to us in some way through some method, to reveal to us the purpose for our creation.

The truth is, we do not seek God nearly as much as God seeks us. The Bible tells us, "We love him, because he first loved us"

(1 JOHN 4:19). God reaches out to us in the ways we are most likely to hear Him and He says to us, "I love you. I created you to have a relationship with Me. I sent Jesus to make that relationship possible for all eternity. I have given you abilities and desires that I intend for you to develop and use, for your fulfillment and for the betterment of mankind."

The messages of God to us are as individualized and unique as we are. They are also as eternal and absolute as God is.

In the previous chapter, I shared with you my belief that God does not change, and His principles do not change. God's messages to us bear the timeless quality of God's own nature.

At the same time, God's *methods* are always subject to innovation and change. God's messages to us are uniquely *for us* when it comes to specific details.

There is a balance between the two and I believe it is important for you to see this balance in order for you to understand how the messages of God to a man named Oral Roberts have direct bearing on *your* life.

When I first discussed with a person in publishing the possibilities for this book, I wasn't sure I had all that much to say. This editor replied, "I understand that. From your perspective, God spoke, you obeyed, and the results speak for themselves."

I said, "Exactly right!"

Then the editor went on to say, "The readers of your book, however, are going to ask, 'What's in it for me?' They want to know how *they* can hear God's voice and what He is likely to say to them."

I also understood that completely. It's the way I'd approach reading a book in which someone else told me about his or her experiences in hearing God's voice. I'd want to know what God was trying to tell **me**.

So, let me tell you what's in the experiences of Oral Roberts for *you.*

Discerning the Difference between Concepts and Applications

First, I believe it is vitally important that you understand very clearly the difference between CONCEPTS and APPLICATIONS.

- CONCEPTS or principles are absolute, eternal, and transcend time, space, and personal differences. They are universal.

- APPLICATIONS are specific, bound to time and space, and are highly personalized. They are unique.

How does this apply to you?

First, everything that God has said in CONCEPT to me, He desires to say to you, and either has said or will say to you. The Bible tells us that God deals with mankind "without partiality"—without playing favorites or showing preference. (SEE ACTS 10:34.) The CONCEPTS of God are for every person. These concepts include God's commandments, His promises, and anything that God says about Himself as Father, Son, and Holy Spirit.

God does not give one revelation of Himself to one person, and a different revelation to another person. His revelation of Himself is the same across all races, all cultures, and in all eons of time.

God does not change and therefore, what He reveals about Himself as God the Father is the same as what He reveals about Himself as God the Son, and both are in complete agreement with what He reveals about Himself as God the Holy Spirit. The nature of God in the Trinity reflects one identity of character and purpose, played out in different roles.

God does not give one set of commandments to one person or group of people, and then give a different set of commandments to another group or person. God's commandments apply to all people, for all time, without regard to race, culture, or nationality.

God does not give one set of promises to one person or group, and then either withhold or enlarge that set of promises to others. God's promises are for all people, in the past and in the present, regardless of race, culture, or nationality. His "conditional" promises apply conditionally the same. His "unconditional" promises apply universally.

Second, what God has said in specific APPLICATION to me, He meant for me. God has specific applications of His concepts for *your life*. God will speak to you about how *you* are to do things, with whom, when, and for what purposes. He will speak to you about *your* talents, *your* relationships, and *your* work and ministry. He will speak to you about the time in which you live, the circle of influence you are to have, and the methods that are right for the message He desires to convey through you.

The conceptual truths God has spoken to me through the years *are* for you because they are rooted in the nature of God.

The specific applications of God's concepts spoken to me were for me alone, just as God will have unique and wonderful applications for you alone.

Three Great Categories of Messages from God

The CONCEPTS that God conveys to His people tend to cluster in three areas:

- God tells us about the relationship He desires to have with us.

- God tells us what He desires to do on our behalf.

- God challenges us to do what He created us to do and to accomplish on the earth.

Let me explore each of these areas briefly with you, recognizing at the outset of our discussion that these areas overlap in some ways.

1. God seeks to establish relationship.

God the Father sent His only Son, Jesus, into this world so that every person who believes in Him might be forgiven and come into right relationship with their Creator.

Jesus not only taught us by word and example *how* God desires for us to live, but through His death on the cross He became the *means* for us to come into close, intimate, unending relationship with God.

Jesus came to restore what Adam and Eve lost through their sin in the Garden of Eden. As I have preached for years, Jesus came to put into us what the devil has tried to take out of us, to take off of us what the devil has tried to put on us, to pull out of us what the devil has sought to put into us, and to lift us out of the circumstances in which the devil has tried to defeat us.

Jesus said the Holy Spirit would be poured out on all people so that He might convict people of their sin, convince people of the right way to live, and make people very aware that they must make a decision about Jesus. (SEE JOHN 16:13.) Everything the Holy Spirit says to us is couched in terms of who Jesus desires to be in His relationship with us:

- He is our Savior, the One who saves us from the deadly consequences of sin.

- He is our Lord, the One who leads us into right paths on a day-to-day basis.

- He is our Deliverer from all evil.

- He is the Rock on which we stand firm and confident.

- He is the Light that reveals truth to us.

- He is the Door through which we pass from death to life.

- He is the Good Shepherd who leads us into green pastures and beside still waters, so that all of our needs are met, we are safe, and our souls are restored.

- He is the Way, the Truth, and the Life.

The Bible gives us hundreds of attributes and names for Jesus, and for God the Father and God the Holy Spirit. All of those words and phrases, taken as a whole, describe the ways in which God desires to *relate* to us. They speak to us of deep and abiding friendship—a friendship that is closer than that of any blood relation and a friendship that never ends. They speak to us of a lasting and loving relationship, which cannot be broken once it has been fully established.

The Bible tells us, "Behold, what manner of love the Father hath bestowed upon us, that we should be called the sons of God.... Beloved, now are we the sons of God, and it doth not yet appear what we shall be: but we know that, when he shall appear, we shall be like him; for we shall see him as he is" (1 JOHN 3:1–2). God has spoken through a number of writers of the New Testament to tell us that we who have believed in Jesus are God's children, joint heirs with Christ of all that God the Father possesses, and that He desires to live with us *forever*.

The relationship to which God calls us is both familial and eternal. God is our Father, Jesus is our elder Brother, the Spirit is our constant companion. Not only today and tomorrow, but *forever*.

The words that God speaks to your heart—by whatever means He chooses—are words that ultimately speak to the RELATIONSHIP that God desires to have with you.

2. God assures us that He is our Source of total supply.

In the late 1960s, God led me to a deep understanding that He alone is our Source of total supply. Name anything that you need to sustain life, and beyond that, to have a life of high quality and purpose, and you must ultimately conclude that God is the Source of what you need.

You cannot cause your heart to beat another beat. You cannot cause your lungs to breathe another breath. You cannot save

yourself. You cannot make yourself whole. You cannot provide all that you need at all times in order to do all that you desire to do!

God alone is your Source of supply of all things that promote life, health, wholeness, love, and joy.

You cannot make the miracle that you need for your present need. Only God can design and send that miracle to you.

You cannot force another person to love you, nor can you force any person to believe in you. Only God can move the human heart.

You cannot by any method have your way all the time and in all circumstances, ensuring all of the outcomes that you desire. Only God has full power to produce eternal results.

The best we human beings can do is put ourselves into position to receive from God by doing what He commands us to do, and to open our lives to receiving all that He desires to give us.

The Bible tells us that God is our Provider and Protector. He gives us all things we need to fulfill the purposes for which He made us.

The good news is that God not only provides for us once and occasionally, He provides for us *always*. God not only protects us from the assaults of evil against our eternal spirit now and again, but *continually*. What God does for us no human being can do, and no human being can undo. Neither can the devil undo what God does in a human heart.

God is the great I AM.

When God commanded Moses to go to Pharaoh and secure the release of the children of Israel out of Egypt, Moses asked the voice that spoke to him from a burning bush, "Behold, when I come unto the children of Israel, and shall say unto them, The God of your fathers hath sent me unto you; and they shall say to me, What is his name? what shall I say unto them?" And God replied to Moses, "I AM THAT I AM: and he said, Thus shalt thou say unto the children of Israel, I AM hath sent me unto you." (SEE EXODUS 3:13–14.)

God is who He declares Himself to be.

God defines Himself.

I look at our world today and I see numerous men and women trying to define who God is. They are attempting to create God to be who they want Him to be and to do what they want Him to do. Some say, "My God would or wouldn't do thus and so." Others say, "The way I see God, He is…"

They might as well try to say they have the power to spin the galaxies or demand that the waves of the ocean cease to roll. God is all-encompassing and self-defining. He creates *us*. We don't create Him. He defines our lives. We don't define Him.

God is the great I AM. He is more than the sum of all the words and phrases He has used to express His identity to us. He is infinite in His presence, wisdom, power, and love. Whatever He has been, He is now and always will be. He is in every moment for all eternity and I have no doubt that as infinite and almighty God, He can and does speak to every person about Himself. Even the most primitive peoples of the earth have an intuitive inner sense that God exists and that He is worthy of worship.

The words that God speaks to you and to me will ultimately be words that tell us more about the nature of God.

God speaks to us to remind us that He created us for His pleasure and purposes. He reminds us that He is sovereign over all things in our lives—He is the beginning and ending of our lives. He reminds us that He is in control of every second of our existence.

We may *think* we are in control, or that some outside force is in control at times. The truth is, God is in control and He is within every circumstance, every situation, every relationship, every opportunity, and every moment, seeking to do His will in us and through us.

God moves to provide us all things that we need, in order to do all things He requires of us. God is a need-meeting God. He knows our needs even before we do, and He has already moved to meet our needs in a way that only He can.

The CONCEPTS of God—His commandments, His promises, His names and attributes—reveal to us more about the great I AM of our lives, the God who never leaves us nor forsakes us even for a moment.

Listen for God to reveal HIMSELF to you.

3. God reveals to us who we are and why we exist.

Finally, when God speaks to us, He ultimately challenges us in some way to do what He created us to do on this earth. He reveals to us our purpose in life.

First, God tells us who He has created us to BE.

He tells us the character traits He desires to produce in us by His Spirit. (SEE GALATIANS 5:22–23.) He tells us the gifts He desires to pour through us for the benefit of others. (SEE ROMANS 12:1–8 AND 1 CORINTHIANS 12.) God reveals to us the innate talents that He has placed within us. He gives us an understanding of ourselves. He shows us our distinctive personality traits.

Do you really know yourself?

Ask God to speak to you about how HE sees you.

Very early in my life, I knew that I had a good mind and that I was far more rational than emotional. Some who have observed my ministry through the years, but who have never taken the time or made the effort to truly get to know me, have seen the heightened emotions of people who are healed, or they have heard the fervor of my early sermons, and they have concluded that I am a person easily swayed by or led by emotions—either mine or the display of emotions in other people. They couldn't be more wrong. My mind quickly moves to bring order to concepts and to seek understanding for the things I perceive. My emotions tend to lag behind what I come to believe through spiritual discernment, study, and learning.

I knew from my childhood that I had an insatiable desire to learn and to study. I knew from my childhood that God had made me with a strong mind and memory, and I believed He intended for me to use my mind and to trust Him for great ideas, great concepts, and great ways of communicating the gospel.

I believe God still desires for me to learn and to study. I am ninety years old as I write this book, but my eyesight is good and I read fifteen to twenty books a month, most of them nonfiction. I am fascinated by eyewitness accounts of history, the personal life stories of people who have overcome great obstacles, and the stories of how certain institutions or laws have become established in our nation.

Very early in my life, I knew the value of faith and recognized that I was a person who had a storehouse of faith that was lying dormant within me. I had living role models of faith in my mother and father. I saw my parents believe for the next sack of groceries so that we might have our next meal. I saw my parents believe for the healing of other people's children. I heard them voice their belief that God was in the process of working miracles, no matter how bleak outward circumstances might appear. One of my favorite spiritual exercises through the years has been to say to myself repeatedly, "By faith! By faith! By faith!" I know what suffering and hardship are. I know what sickness and desire are. I know what a life of sin is. I know what it is to dream of going high in this world against all odds of success. And I know that faith makes a difference, not just some of the time, but all of the time. It is BY FAITH that God calls each of us to live. It is BY FAITH that we follow God, live in health, have energy and strength, have the ability to learn and work, and fulfill the purpose He has for us.

Very early in my life, I knew I had a compassion for people who were sick. Long before I entered the healing ministry, I had nearly overwhelming impulses to rush to the side of people who were in physical trouble or ailment. I wanted to rip disease from their

bodies, straighten their twisted limbs, or take away whatever was limiting them in any way. I was troubled any time I was held back from doing so.

Very early in my life, I knew I had a strong will. I may not always have used that will in the most gentle ways, but I have always had a strong understanding of right and wrong, good and evil, and I have turned my will toward what I believe is right and good.

I have chosen to do what God has chosen for me. I have turned my will toward obeying God.

Of course I was tempted throughout my life—just as every human being is tempted. The truth is that every person is tempted, no matter how strong that person may be spiritually. We never mature to the point that we are beyond temptation. Even so, I chose to obey God's commands. Obedience is by our *will*.

I was one hundred percent faithful to my darling wife Evelyn all the years of our marriage. I gave everything to the projects God called me to build, giving far more money than I ever kept for myself—I was never in the ministry for money. When I learned through the years that I was not following good health practices, I learned how to eat for greater health and vitality, I began to control my weight and to exercise regularly, and I learned how to change the way I preached to protect my voice so that I didn't destroy it by loud yelling. I'm neither bragging nor complaining, I am simply telling you that some things happen in life because we set our *will* toward making them happen. I know the power of the human will to say "yes" to God and "no" to the devil. I know that we *CAN* do many things we have never thought we could do *IF* we will exercise our faith and our will as God speaks to us and leads us.

I am telling you all this to say, I know Oral Roberts better than any person knows me or will ever know me. I know myself because God has told me who I am in His eyes and from His perspective. He has revealed to me how He made me, why He made me, and the purposes for which I am alive—even to this present day. He has shown me the areas of weakness I must avoid or trust Him to strengthen. He has shown me the areas of my strength that I must not misuse in dealing with other people.

I have discovered through the years that an amazing thing happens when God reveals to us who we are. He gives us an understanding of ourselves with this affirmation to our spirit: "I made you this way for a purpose. I love you just the way I created you." When God reveals to us who we are, we are able to accept ourselves even as we seek to improve ourselves, and we have a better ability to accept others even as we attempt to help them to help themselves.

Second, God speaks to us about how we are to LIVE and BEHAVE.

God very clearly gives us guidelines for how we are to live our lives, regardless of the specific tasks and projects He gives us to complete. For example:

- God always calls us to deal honestly with other people.

- God always calls us to speak the truth as we fulfill our purpose on the earth.

- God calls us to be givers, not takers—receivers, but neither "graspers" nor "users."

- God calls us to be yoked with those who are of like mind and heart, and to refrain from committed associations with unbelievers.

- God calls us to keep the Ten Commandments—to refrain from adultery, lying, stealing, coveting, false witness, and to actively worship the Lord God, keep His Sabbath days, and honor our parents.

- God calls us to turn from evil and toward good—in all situations.

God's eternal and unchanging truths tell us *how* to live a life that is pleasing to God. They reveal to us right and wrong. They give us clarity about what is truly helpful and what is harmful.

The truths about the *way* in which He wants us to live are vital for our success. I am firmly convinced that no person can succeed beyond the degree to which he or she is willing to obey what God has commanded. Why? Because all of the commandments are for our good. Obedience to God, including the keeping of His commandments, puts us into position for reward and blessing. God wants to give us miracles—but He also wants us to be in the precise position to receive His miracles.

When God speaks to you about His eternal CONCEPTS, He will very often focus on speaking to you about who you are to BE, and HOW YOU ARE TO LIVE in right relationship with Him.

In the end, what God reveals to us about ourselves and the way in which we are to live sets us up to gain an understanding of what *specifically* God wants us to accomplish.

Seven Supreme Qualities about God's Messages to Us

Finally, there are seven supreme qualities about God's messages to us that are important for you to consider as you read the coming chapters.

1. God will always speak to you in a way that challenges you to change, grow, or develop in some way.

God always calls us to be and do *more*—to reach higher, believe for even greater things, and to pursue even nobler goals. God is never content with your status quo. The truth is, your status quo is far below your God-given potential! God calls you to be *all* and to do *all* that He designed for you.

Trust me on this: I have searched God's Word thoroughly and there isn't one place where God says, "Go sit in a rocking chair and rock away your days." The word "retirement" is not in the Bible. Neither is the phrase, "Kick back, relax, and watch life go by."

2. God will always speak to you in ways that you understand what He is saying.

God does not give us riddles. He doesn't pose questions for which there are no answers. He doesn't play games with us. When God speaks to you, you will know clearly what He is saying—you won't have to question whether you heard Him accurately.

If you have any doubt that you have heard Him clearly, ask Him about what you have heard.

If you have any doubt that you are to seek a particular path to pursue, ask Him to give you additional input.

If you have any doubt that you are to go through a particular door or accept a particular opportunity, ask Him for additional guidance.

Jesus taught His followers, "Ask, and it shall be given you; seek, and ye shall find; knock, and it shall be opened unto you" (MATTHEW 7:7). God will not speak to you and leave you scratching your head. He is more than willing to help you understand His intentions fully and accurately.

Now, God may not give you all the details. Many times God expects us to put our lives and faith into motion before He unfolds details to us. But, God will give you the guidance you need to get started!

3. God will always speak to you in ways that allow you to "put to the test" or to verify the truth of what He is speaking to you.

God does not speak to us in pie-in-the-sky terminology. He is immensely practical. His commands, promises, and revelations about Himself have real-world applications.

**4. God will never tell you to be something
or do something that is contrary to what
you will find in the Bible, or what you will see
in the lives of truly godly people through the ages.**

God doesn't contradict Himself.

5. God's messages to us always have a ring of eternity about them.

We know that what God is saying to us is either an eternal truth—about our relationship with Him, His nature, or His purposes for us—or that it will lead to eternal consequences and fruit, in our lives or the lives of others. Nothing about the messages of God to us is for our self-serving pleasure or advancement. His messages to us are always about what is best *forever*, for us and for all others called by His name.

6. All of God's messages to us point eventually to Jesus.

God's messages direct our attention toward who we are in Christ Jesus and who He is to us. They aim us toward what Jesus has done for us and made possible for us. They point toward what we are to do to bring greater glory to His name and to extend His kingdom on this earth.

If you don't see Jesus clearly in what you believe God is speaking to you, it isn't God who is speaking. The Holy Spirit of God speaking in your spirit always testifies of Jesus and glorifies Him.

The Bible commands us to test what we hear in our spirits. We are challenged to have sharp discernment, and to put every message we hear to this test: Does it result in exalting Jesus? (SEE 1 JOHN 4:1–3.) God always speaks to us so that we might bring glory to Christ Jesus, now and forever.

7. God's messages have an "other than me" quality about them.

God uses words and phraseology that are distinct and unusual. He nearly always expresses Himself in ways a person hasn't thought about, dreamed about, or intended.

If you find yourself saying after hearing from God, "Well, that's just what I thought God would say"...you may not have been hearing God's voice. You may have been merely reinforcing your own ideas.

God speaks to us something that is BEYOND our own finite self. He speaks to us from the infinite realm of His eternity and holiness. He is not an echo in our minds, He is an initiator of something new that He implants in us.

Look for God to Confirm His Word

One of the great principles of the Bible is that God *confirms* the truth of His word out of the mouth of two or three witnesses. (SEE DEUTERONOMY 17:6, 19:15, AND 2 CORINTHIANS 13:1 AS EXAMPLES.)

When God speaks to you, your first response should be to say, "Yes, Lord."

And your second response should be to listen closely for the ways in which God confirms that word to you. He may speak the same message to you a second time—or many times. He may cause the thoughts and meaning of His message to so fill your mind day after day, week after week, month after month, that you cannot escape His message. He may cause you to hear a song that confirms the word of the Lord to you, or put you into position to hear a sermon, or to read a passage of the Bible that *directly* confirms that God has spoken to you in your spirit.

It is not enough to hear God speak to you once. Listen for the repeated messages of His truth in you and all around you. God *will* confirm what He says to you.

It is in this way that God keeps us from acting on human whim. Confirmation is His method for guiding us to the very heart of His will.

God's Messages to Me and What They Mean to You

CHAPTER FIVE

More than Ready to Hear

Hearing the truth ABOUT God prepared my heart to hear FROM God.

LORD, thou hast heard the desire of the humble:

thou wilt prepare their heart.

—PSALM 10:17

he year was 1935. I was seventeen years old and I was dying faster than I was living. Only a year before, I had high hopes for my life, but at this point, I truly believed what I was saying when I told my father, "Papa, I've gone the last mile of the way."

I had tuberculosis in both lungs.

The diagnosis had been like a sledgehammer to my soul. When my father conveyed to me what the physicians had told him, I felt as if my entire world came crashing down around me. Black despair flooded into my soul.

Momma was half-blood Cherokee and tuberculosis seemed to be especially rampant among the Indian communities in Oklahoma in those days. Both my mother's father and one of her sisters had died with tuberculosis—both of them when they were quite young. The "miracle drugs" that were able to cure tuberculosis were still years away from full development and use. It was common knowledge in the rural community in which I lived that when people took TB, they didn't get well. I had no hope that my outcome would be any different. It seemed to be the "fate" of Oral Roberts to die from tuberculosis.

I was bedfast for one hundred sixty-three days.

I coughed and spit up blood and tossed on my bed day and night, not able to sleep more than a few hours at a time. I went as long as forty-eight hours without a wink of sleep. Food lost its taste and I became a pile of skin and bones on a six-foot, one-inch frame. My weight dropped from one hundred sixty pounds to one hundred twenty pounds.

I sometimes screamed at the sharp pain that seemed to pierce my lungs like daggers. I was not ashamed to cry, although crying only made my coughing worse.

Apart from my physical condition, I was sick in my soul, and in my spirit. I had no hope and I began to wish for death.

During those days I began to learn some of the strange ideas that people have about God, religion, sickness, and healing. Nearly everybody who came to see me had a remedy, a philosophy, and a theology. I remember vividly the day one of the leading pastors of our city came to call on me. He walked to my bedside, took my hand in his, and said, "Son, be patient. You will just have to be patient with this thing." Then he said a few words of prayer, asking God to make me patient, and he went on his way.

This pastor didn't call upon God to heal my body. He did not give me hope that a miracle from God could save me. He never mentioned the power of faith, nor did he encourage me to believe God for *anything* that I so desperately needed. I remember saying bitterly after he left, "Be patient? What will that get me? When did patience ever heal TB?" Had I remained patient in my disease, I have little doubt that I would have spent many years in a sanatorium or been put in a grave more than seventy years ago.

There were a few religious people who came to see me and concluded during their visit that the Lord had tracked me down and put this awful disease upon me for a purpose only God knew. One Sunday afternoon the house seemed filled with such people. They all had an opinion about my situation, and they all seemed to agree that God had caused me to have TB. One person spoke up and suggested that perhaps somebody with faith could pray and the Lord would heal me. Another one quickly squelched that idea, saying, "How do you know it is God's will to heal him?"

I listened to discussions such as these about the pros and cons of God's healing power and God's will, and I concluded that I didn't have much use for a God who would cause a seventeen-year-old young man to become sick with such a horrible disease.

The church people then seemed to turn to the idea that, while they were not sure if God wanted to heal me, they *were* certain that God wanted to save my soul. People began to pray that God would save me *before I died*.

I thought long and hard about what the religious people had said. As far as I was concerned, they talked out of both sides of their mouths. To them, sickness and salvation both came from the Lord. They believed the best a person could do was endure. There was no

expecting a miracle, no believing that God could change things, and no hope that God could or would bring deliverance to a human life.

I finally had had enough of all that. I told my father that I didn't want to hear any more of what the local church people had to say. I did not believe God loved me and I did not want to get saved if God was the cause of my sickness. I made a decision: "If God put this on me, I don't want to serve Him." I told Papa the church people might as well leave me alone. With a few pious glances (and raised eyebrows, no doubt), the people gladly stopped coming.

The First Sparks of Hope and Faith

I have learned through the years that very often when we are at the lowest point of hope in our lives, God will send someone to help us find our way to Him. In my life, that person was my mother.

One day Momma came to my room, sat down on the bed beside me, and began talking to me about my birth. I had heard the story before, of course. Three months before I was born, Momma had received a call from a neighbor that her child was dying of pneumonia. The doctor had said the infant would not live through the night. The parents called for Momma to come and pray. It was a two-mile walk across the fields and late in the evening, but Momma went. Along the way she came to a barbed-wire fence. Carefully parting the strands of wire, she crawled through, tired, alone, and awkward in her sixth month of pregnancy. Her dress got caught and as she stood there in the blowing wind of that desolate prairie pasture, she said, "God, I want to make a vow. I ask You to heal my neighbor's child tonight, and when mine is born, I will give him to You."

Upon arriving at the neighbor's house, Momma said to the father of the sick child these words of faith: "God will heal your child." She then went over and put her hand on the child and prayed in the name of Christ Jesus. The baby lived and that settled the matter for Momma.

The baby she was carrying would be a boy, and a preacher. She asked for confirmation of her vow—she prayed for a blue-eyed boy. Sure enough, unlike my parents and all of my siblings, my eyes are blue.

From Momma's perspective, her son Oral couldn't die from tuberculosis. He was called to be a preacher and he hadn't yet preached! She reminded me that day as she came to my bedside that I belonged to God and God's hand was on my life.

I said, "Momma, all these people say God put tuberculosis on me."

She said, "Oral, God didn't afflict you."

I said, "Well, Momma, if God didn't, who did?"

She said, "The devil did. He is trying to destroy your life."

I said, "But why?"

She said, "When God calls someone, the devil always tries to destroy him, but if you will give your heart to Jesus and have faith in the Lord, He will raise you up from this bed and heal you."

It was the first time the idea had entered my head that God might heal my body. I knew very well by then that the medicines couldn't and wouldn't heal me. But, I hadn't thought about whether God might. Momma was the first person to plant a seed of faith and hope in my heart.

My sister Jewel came to visit us about a week later. I was the youngest of five children and by the time I became ill, I was the only child left at home. Jewel came straight to my bed, looked down on me, and I could see the tears in her eyes. She told me she had been praying and seeking God. And then suddenly she said, as if she was making an announcement, "Oral, God is going to heal you."

I didn't say anything in reply, but those seven words caused hope to leap inside me. I can still feel it today—those faith-inspiring words that God not only *can*, but God *will* heal.

From that time on the devil was never able to take away hope from my heart.

I still wasn't saved, however.

Papa, Momma, and Jewel had a conference during Jewel's visit and they agreed together that God was going to heal me. Papa went

into action and wrote letters to people who he knew had faith in the Lord's power to heal. He wrote to churches, preachers, and other Christians, saying, "Pray for Oral to be healed."

Late one night a car drove up into our front yard and we heard voices call out, "Brother Roberts! Brother Roberts! The Lindsay saints are here!"

These midnight callers were from Lindsay, Oklahoma. They were long-time friends of Papa and Momma, and my parents rejoiced at their arrival. They took little time in starting their own praise service. Then they said, "Where is Oral?"

Papa led them to my bed and they gathered around. I looked up into their bright faces and every one of them had a shining countenance. Every one of them stood with hope and every one of them knew how to pray!

I had heard lots of prayers in the preceding weeks, but none of them ever stirred me all the way to the depths of my soul. These folks from Lindsay were different. They lifted their hands and I heard them pray strong, bold prayers filled with hope, joy, and faith. My spirit drank in everything these "Lindsay saints" said and I was so thrilled at their praying and their joy that I believe, in retrospect, I could have been healed in that moment if only I had known more fully how to receive their prayers and release my faith.

When they left at daybreak I said to my father, "Papa, when I get religion, I want the kind those people have."

More than a Need for Physical Healing

I was not in right relationship with God and I was dying with tuberculosis, but these weren't the only problems I had! I also stuttered and stammered so severely that I could hardly say my name.

Because of that, the words of my mother about my becoming a preacher tended to fall on unbelieving ears. Papa came to me one day before I became sick. He wanted to give me a personal word of prophecy about my life. I remember his words as clearly as if he had spoken them yesterday. He looked into my eyes and said, "Oral, someday you will be a preacher. God will give you the largest meetings of your day. They will be so large, others will go before you and prepare the way. All you will have to do is go preach and minister to the people."

I remember staring at him blankly and saying, "Papa, what in the world are you talking about?"

He said, "Son, I am talking about you. The hand of God is upon your life and you will see these things come to pass."

I said, "Papa, I can't even talk. I stutter and stammer so bad that I wish I didn't even have to go to school."

Papa said, "Mark my words. It will come to pass."

Virtually nobody else thought so. The Roberts relatives had very little regard for me. My next older brother Vaden was the one everybody thought had a bright future, and possibly a bright future as a preacher. Vaden always had a wonderful outgoing personality and he was the favorite of our kinfolks. For that matter, he was also my favorite. When people looked at the two of us, they'd say, "Here is the one who is going to make a mark," and they pointed to Vaden.

Vaden and I seemed opposites. I was frail in body. Vaden was robust and strong.

I stuttered and stammered. Vaden could always talk his way out of a jam and make people laugh to the point they wanted to do for him and with him whatever he desired.

I tended to hang back in any crowd. Vaden stepped forward and led.

It was a good thing for me that Vaden always stood up for me. When the neighborhood boys taunted me, the students at school laughed at me, or when the neighborhood bully punched me and tried to make me talk, Vaden came to my defense.

When I got sick, Vaden said to God, "Put the TB on me, God. I can take it. Oral has always been weak. Put it on me." You can't put a value on that kind of love.

Vaden was quite willing, also, for me to become the preacher among the children of Claudius and E.M. Roberts. He certainly didn't want that job for himself.

And so it was—no matter how much Papa believed I would one day be a preacher, and no matter how much Momma believed I had been called from before my birth to be a minister of the gospel, and no matter how much my older brother was willing for me to be a preacher...I had no sense whatsoever that I would ever actually be a preacher. Nor did I want to be one.

I had much different aspirations. I wanted to become a lawyer, and perhaps one day enter politics and become governor of the state of Oklahoma. Mostly I wanted to be educated and to pursue a life of service.

I was sixteen when I started to see the walls close in on me. I recalled that as soon as my older brothers had reached an age when my father thought they were sufficiently educated, they were sent out into the world to earn their own living. I could see that time coming—fast. While I had no aversion to working, I wanted to finish high school and go on to college.

About that same time the basketball coach at my high school, who was a real mentor to me in many ways, accepted a job at a school in a town about fifty miles away. Knowing my situation and my dreams for more education, he asked me if I wanted to make the move also. I told him I did and when my parents discerned what I was about to do, Papa intercepted me and said, "Oral, I will put every policeman in Oklahoma on your trail." I replied, "Papa, go right ahead. As many times as you bring me back I will run away again." He saw that I meant to leave. I packed my clothes and as I was doing so, Momma came to me and said, "Oral, you may be able to get away from us but you won't be able to get away from our prayers. We want you to remember one thing. Every day that you are gone we will be calling your name to the Lord and we won't stop praying until the Lord brings you back home."

I paid little attention to what either of them said. I never considered the heartache and the sorrow I was bringing to them. All I could see was a brighter future and a fresh start ahead of me—fifty miles away at a school where I might not be laughed at, where I'd have a chance to learn, and where I could live a new life that had nothing to do with the poverty of my family and the strict religious atmosphere of my church. I felt fully ready to live life on my own terms.

The afternoon I left Ada, my coach and I were riding together in his car when he suddenly pulled over to the side of the road, stopped, handed me the keys, and said, "You drive." I had never driven a car before but I felt I *should* be able to do it if I put my mind to it. I had certainly watched other people drive! We both got out of the car and exchanged places and I began to drive. Badly. But after a few minutes of lurching and swerving, I got the hang of the clutch and shifting gears and steering. As I look back on it, I think my coach never wanted it said that *he* had forced me to leave by driving me away. He put the situation squarely in my hands so that I would know and anybody else who saw what was happening would know that I was driving myself away from my past and toward my future.

I rented a room in my new location and got a job as a newspaper reporter. I quickly discovered that I needed several small jobs if I was going to have enough money to pay for my lodging, food, clothes, shoes, and other necessities. I enrolled in school and made the basketball team. I studied hard.

One of my jobs was to stoke the fires in the place where I was living, which happened to be the home of a former judge. I felt drawn to this man's library, and after basketball practice, work, and homework, I often stayed up into the early morning hours reading voraciously from the large leather-bound books that lined those library walls.

Many days I didn't eat enough; many nights I only got two or three hours of sleep. I began to feel weak. On a few nights, I awoke in the middle of the night with a hot fever, coughing and spitting up blood. I never thought about going back home, however.

In the midst of all this, I had told God to get out of my life. And He did.

It's a scary thing when a person says to God, "Leave me alone." He doesn't violate our human will. He does what we ask, and we quickly discover just how much trouble we can get into when we choose to live life solely on our own terms. I found myself on a mad and sinful merry-go-round of my own making.

Then one night during the state basketball tournament I collapsed on the basketball court. Someone picked me up and carried me into the locker room and helped me change into my street clothes. My coach found me there after the game and said, "Son, you are going home." He put me in his car and drove me back to Ada. There, he helped me out of the car and into the house where he said to my father, "Reverend Roberts, I have brought your boy home."

Papa and Momma took one look at me and began to cry. They helped me into bed.

A short time after I had returned home, Papa and Momma moved to Stratford, Oklahoma, about eighteen miles from Ada. Papa had been called to pastor a church there. I improved a little and was able to stand for a few hours at a time. But, that didn't last long. When I collapsed the second time, I was bedfast over five months.

One night, Papa came to my room on what was the "prayer-meeting night" at the church. He said, "Oral, I am not going to prayer meeting tonight. I have asked someone to take the service."

I said, "What's the matter, Papa?"

He said, "Son, I am going to kneel by your bed tonight and pray. I am not going to get off my knees until you get saved and give your heart to God."

He called Momma and the nurse and they all began to pray. In a few minutes Momma and the nurse finished their prayers and got up, but Papa had just started to pray. I found myself listening closely to what he said and I began to feel something stirring deep inside me. I looked up into his face, and in that moment, I had a vision. It was as clear as anything I have ever seen with my natural eyes. I saw the face of Jesus in Papa's face.

I had never really wanted to be saved before that moment, but suddenly I began to cry. My heart was broken into a thousand pieces, and pretty soon I was asking God to save my soul. I told the Lord that if He would save me, I would give Him my life, what little of it there was left. I said to the Lord, "Jesus, I have nothing to offer You. My health is gone. My body is wrecked. I have nothing left. But if You will save me, I will give You what I have."

I felt God's presence strike my feet and move slowly up through my legs. In a matter of seconds the powerful presence of God began surging throughout my entire being. My face began to shine and I cried out to Papa, "Look at this light on my face." I felt as light as a feather and so happy I wanted to shout at the top of my voice. The power of God inside me built to such intensity that it lifted me up and I found myself standing in the bed with my hands upraised, praising and magnifying God and saying, "I am saved! I am saved! I am saved!"

I didn't know it fully at the time, but that night was the move that truly put me in the right position to hear from God and to receive my healing. The presence of God was so strong in me that night that had I known then what I know now, I truly believe I could have received my healing that night *directly from God.* I didn't know, however, so again, I was flat on my back by the next morning. I was saved and that was eternally important, but I was not healed.

Moving to "Prime Position" for Hearing from God

Up to that point in my life and my illness, I had heard the truth *about* God. That is a very good thing and I do not discount hearing the truth *about* God in the least. But, it is not the same as hearing *directly from* God.

Some people say they hear from the Lord through the prophetic words, and words of wisdom and knowledge other people speak.

That may be their experience, and I do believe that is more likely true for those who are already saved than for those who are not. But in my life...

The prophetic words of my mother and father turned my heart toward God and toward a belief that God had a plan and purpose for my life. They sparked a glimmer of hope in me that God might heal me directly.

The inspiring faith-filled words of my sister Jewel unleashed a flood of hope in my heart.

The prayers of the "Lindsay saints" and others who had faith helped me *want* God in my life.

But none of these words from others were the same as hearing directly from God.

My accepting Jesus as my personal Savior was the final step for me to be in right relationship with God. It was the step across the threshold for me personally to enter *fully* into His presence. And, I believe it was a necessary step for me to take so that I would be in what I call "PRIME POSITION" for hearing His voice and receiving His healing power.

Things began to happen very quickly from that night of my salvation onward.

And believe me, I was a young man more than ready to hear what God was about to say.

Evaluate Your Own Heart

Have you accepted Jesus as your personal Savior?

Do you feel a stirring in you to believe God for an area of your life that you know needs to be healed or changed?

Do you want God's guidance for your life and direction for your future?

Listen.

And listen again.

Listen today.

CHAPTER SIX

God's First Words to Me

They changed my life.
And they can change yours.

I will hear what God the LORD will speak:
for he will speak peace [wholeness] unto
his people, and to his saints.
—PSALM 85:8

Two or three weeks after I accepted Jesus as my Savior, an evangelist named George Moncey brought his big tent to Ada, Oklahoma. Elmer, my oldest brother, lived at Ada and went out to hear this man preach. He was astounded at what he heard and the miracles he saw. The entire town was stirred. People were bringing their sick from distant places in Oklahoma to have this man pray for them.

All his life Elmer had believed in divine healing because Momma and Papa had taught him to believe. He had seen people healed when he was a child, but he hadn't witnessed much in the way of healing miracles since he had become an adult. One night when he got home from the tent meeting, he said to his wife, "Orie, how much money do we have before payday?"

She replied, "Elmer, we only have thirty-five cents."

He said, "Let me have it. I am going to borrow a car and go to Stratford tomorrow and get Oral. If I can bring him here to the tent so Brother Moncey can pray for him, I believe the Lord will heal his body."

And that's what happened. Elmer borrowed a car, put thirty-five cents' worth of gas in it, and came to get me. I heard the car drive up to our house and almost immediately, Elmer seemed to be at my bedside, saying, "Oral, get up! God is going to heal you!"

I said, "Elmer, is He really going to heal me?"

He said, "Yes, He is. Get up out of that bed. I am taking you over to the big tent in Ada and Brother Moncey will pray for you."

I said, "Elmer, I can't get up."

He said, "Then I will carry you."

Momma began to shout and rejoice at what Elmer was doing as he helped me get dressed and then, with Papa's help, carried me out to the car and helped me lie down on a mattress that had been placed in the back seat. Elmer, Papa, and Momma got in the front seat and away we drove.

As we made our way to Ada, I began to listen to what I could hear of the conversation in the front seat. Elmer was recounting various miracles he had witnessed and in my mind's eye, I could see vividly what he was describing. I had no doubt that what he told Momma and Papa was the truth. I believed every word of it.

Then suddenly everything grew very quiet and still. I seemed to be lying in a pool of absolute silence. There wasn't even the sound of the car traveling down the road. A voice called my name: "Oral Roberts! Oral Roberts!" The sound of it both startled and scared me, for I had never heard a voice like it. Then in an instant I knew it was God. I had never heard His voice before but I knew without any doubt that I was hearing the voice of God. He said:

> "Son, I am going to heal you, and you are to
> take My healing power to your generation."

My flesh tingled as God spoke those same words to me three times, and then I heard no more. The former sounds of the road and the voices of my brother and parents returned.

Even before I had heard God's voice, I believed I was going to be healed. Now I knew with *certainty* that I would be healed and just as importantly, *why*.

Loosed and Set Free

When we arrived at the tent, there was a great crowd. I was put in a rocking chair with pillows at my sides and back. Soon, Brother Moncey began preaching. I had never seen him before that night, and never saw him after, but I remember that he was a fairly heavy-set man who seemed very friendly toward the people. He preached over an hour, made an altar call, and then he began to pray for people to be healed. Just before he prayed for me, he came to where I was sitting, in part to greet my father as a fellow minister. He said, "The other night I prayed for a boy about your age with tuberculosis, an Indian boy, and the Lord healed him instantly. You just look up and believe. The Lord will heal you tonight."

I told him I would do what he said.

About eleven o'clock at night, my turn came in the prayer line. Momma and Papa helped me up and almost carried me to Brother Moncey because I was so weak. His prayer for me may have lasted ten seconds...but it was powerful.

I had become accustomed to people praying, "Oh, Lord, please do this and do that." Brother Moncey didn't pray like that. He put his hands on my head and seemed to be speaking to some unseen power of evil and disease, and he literally *commanded* the tuberculosis to come out of me. He said, "Thou cursed disease, I command you in the name of Jesus Christ to come out of this boy's lungs. Loose him, and let him go."

Something struck my lungs, and I began tingling throughout my entire body. A beautiful light engulfed me, and the next thing I knew, I was racing back and forth on the platform with my hands raised, shouting at the top of my voice, "I am healed! I am healed! I am healed!"

We had lived in Ada for a number of years and most of the people in the audience knew my parents and about my having tuberculosis. The power of God struck that audience about the same time it struck my lungs. As I began racing up and down, the crowd leaped to its feet, some ran down the aisles, some waved their handkerchiefs, and some fell on their knees and began to pray. Papa later told me that more than a thousand people were shouting and praising God at the same time.

Brother Moncey came over and led me to the microphone, put it in my hands, and said, "Son, tell the people what the Lord has done for you."

I took that microphone in my hands and spoke to that crowd as if I had spent half my life on the public platform. My tongue was loosed. There was no stuttering or stammering. I had absolutely no fear of the crowd. The words tumbled out of me as I told them how Jesus Christ of Nazareth had healed my lungs, how I could breathe all the way to the bottom of my lungs without pain or coughing or hemorrhaging. I told them I had been given strength in my entire body to walk up and down the platform. God had healed me from the top of my head to the soles of my feet, and from the inside out.

My brother and parents took me to that meeting on a mattress in the back seat of a borrowed car, but as we went home, I was sitting up and rejoicing every mile of the way.

It took me a while to regain my strength after so much time in bed, but the TB was healed instantly. After I had my lungs fluoroscoped at the Sugg Clinic in Ada, Dr. Morey announced to me, "Just forget you ever had TB. Your lungs are as sound as a dollar."

About two months after my healing, a group of young men from Holmes Bible College in Greenville, South Carolina, came to Oklahoma to hold revival meetings. They invited me to preach with them that summer. Two of the young men—Raymond Corvin, who had been saved in one of Papa's revivals in Center, Oklahoma, and Albert Barfield went one direction, and Simpson A. Merritt and I went to the Homer schoolhouse about four miles east of Ada. We spent a little time out in the woods near the schoolhouse praying, and Simpson announced to me, "Oral, you are going to preach your first sermon tonight." I was too happy to be scared. I agreed and I began hunting for a text of Scripture. I settled on the fourth chapter of Mark in which the story is told of how Jesus was awakened from His sleep in a ship during a storm, and how He rose up and said, "Peace be still," and hushed the raging sea.

Simpson went to the house where we were staying but I stayed in the woods and began to preach to the trees. As I looked at them, I began to see them as if they were people. Having practiced on the trees, I felt confident I could speak to whomever came to the meeting.

That night I preached for about twenty minutes and two people came forward to give their hearts to Jesus Christ. It was the beginning.

At the end of two weeks in that location, an elderly man got up and said that he guessed the people who were meeting in that

schoolhouse should take up an offering to help these two young preachers. They passed the collection plate and gave the entire collection to us. Simpson counted out my half. It was eighty-three cents. The amount didn't really matter. What mattered was that I had been *able* to preach. I had strength. I could talk. God gave me something to say. And souls were won to Christ.

I had entered the ministry.

What God's Words to Me Mean to Your Life Today

God's words to me were profound. They changed everything about both my present and my future. There are three things in what God said to me that are important to *your* life.

1. God called me "Son."

God's first word to me after He got my attention by calling my name, was the most important word I could have ever heard from God, or will ever hear from Him.

He called me SON.

I had accepted Jesus Christ as my Savior, and in so doing, had laid claim to God being my heavenly Father. God confirmed that He, indeed, was proud to be my Father and that we were in eternal, intimate, familial relationship—from that moment for all eternity. He called me *SON*.

The most important truth of your life comes when you know without any shadow of doubt that God is your heavenly Father, and that He has laid claim to you as His beloved child.

Listen for God to call you SON…or DAUGHTER.

What God said to me, He longs to say to you.

God speaks that word to each of us who are truly His children, and in the truth of that word, the most important thing that ever needs to be established in your life becomes established for all eternity. There is no turning back. There is no doubt.

You belong to God.

You are His beloved child.

You are His heir—a joint heir with Jesus Christ.

You are in a position to receive *everything* your loving Father desires to give His child.

2. God told me what He was going to do for me.

God doesn't always tell us *first* what He is going to do for us, but very often He does. The truth is that God is far more desirous of doing for us than most of us are desirous of doing for God.

God said, "I am going to heal you."

As I have reflected on what God said to me over the decades, I have come to see that this was far more than a simple statement.

God told me something about Himself in His words to me.

God said, "I AM." He spoke to me from the full depth of His identity and the full breadth of His power.

The great I AM, who first revealed Himself to Moses by that name, was and is the same great I AM that created the world and all that is in it. God entered the back seat of a borrowed car on a stretch of road between Stratford and Ada, Oklahoma, to say to me—a sick seventeen-year-old boy living on the backside of nowhere—that He, the great I AM, had taken note of me and was going to make me whole.

Can you begin to fathom the truth that the God who created all things, the Almighty King of this universe, cares about *you*—individually, personally, intimately, completely? I'm here to tell you that He does. He loves you beyond measure and He desires to bless you and make you whole, even though you can scarcely take in that truth.

I have no doubt that God desires to reveal Himself to you as the great I AM of your life.

He is there, even if all others fail you.

He is there, even if you don't recognize Him or know Him.

He is there, even if you don't know how to talk to Him.

He is there, closer than the very breath in your body, and He cares for you.

God told me what
He was going to do on my behalf.

God said, "I AM…going to HEAL you."

I knew there was more in me that needed healing than my lungs. My entire body needed healing. My tongue needed healing. My mind needed healing—it needed regeneration. My outlook on life needed healing. My habits needed healing. My desires needed healing. My self-value and feelings of self-worth needed healing. *Everything* about Oral Roberts needed to be changed from weakness to strength, from bad to good, from confusion to confidence. I needed to be lifted up, renewed, and made *whole*.

You need the same thing. There's something in you that isn't whole today—that's true for every person on this planet. There's something lacking or something that isn't functioning correctly or something that is out of balance. God desires to have you hear Him say to you, "I am going to HEAL you."

God is a healing God.

His healing power is for you.

His desire is to make you whole, just as His desire was to make me whole.

There's something that God desires to do on your behalf.

3. "You are to take My healing power to your generation."

God gave me the direction for my entire life in just ten words. He gave me understanding about why He was healing me and even more, why He had created me.

There are two truths in this I don't want you to miss.

God has something for you to do for your generation.

God didn't make you to have you waste your time, talents, or energies on things that are of no use to you or anyone else. He made you to do something that is beyond yourself. He made you to make a difference for good and for God.

I knew intuitively and immediately that God's healing power was whole-person healing power. God didn't call me to walk the halls of hospitals and heal people of their diseases. He called me to preach and teach *wholeness* to people. I knew fully that God was calling me to address all of the "sickness" in any person—to address their spiritual needs, their mental and emotional needs, their financial needs, their physical needs, and their relationship needs.

I knew that when God told me I was to TAKE His healing power to my generation, I was to preach healing, pray healing, and teach healing. And in the teaching, I would eventually establish a university based upon God's healing power. That was part of the *meaning* of God's message to me.

I didn't know how to do what God told me to do.

I didn't even know very much about how to begin to do what God had commanded.

But I knew God had placed a mandate on my life and that He was commanding me to move in a direction that would encompass all of my life, bring fulfillment to all of my days, and give me meaning and purpose no matter how fierce any opposition against me might be.

The truth is that God has something specific for you to do. If you do not know the reason for your life, ask God to speak to you about why He made you and what He wants you to do. He desires to speak to you as clearly as He spoke to me.

**God will call you to become an extension
to others of what He has done in your life.**

The area of your life that God heals and makes whole is very likely the area of service that God wants you to extend to others.

I've seen it more times than I can count.

The person who has been healed emotionally from abuse becomes a healer to others who are abused. The person who has been healed physically becomes a nurse or physician. The person who has been healed psychologically becomes a therapist or counselor. The person who has had a radical conversion becomes the person with a radical heart for winning souls. The person who grew up with a hunger for learning and was given opportunity to learn and develop his mind becomes the master teacher, regardless of subject or craft.

No person can minister God's love to another person beyond his level of personal experience. Not really. You may be able to minister the *truth* of God to another person. But to truly minister God's *love*, the other person must know that you have been where he is at, you've been through what he is going through, and that the way you trusted God is the way he can trust God.

You will find it very difficult to believe for others to have a miracle in any area of their life unless you have experienced that miracle in your own life. The converse is also true: You will find it easy and compelling to believe for miracles in the lives of others once you have experienced miracles!

Could I have become a healing evangelist without having been healed? I don't know. What I do know is that I have been a far more compassionate and effective healing evangelist because I know what it means to have been sick in so many ways, and to know that God can heal *everything* that attempts to defeat, diminish, or destroy a person in any area of his or her life.

Look at what God has done for you. Listen for the way He desires to make you an extension of His work in you. What He has done in you, He very likely desires to do *through* you.

Evaluate Your Own Heart

Are you in right relationship with God today?

Can you call Him Father? Does He call you Son or Daughter?

Do you grasp that God, the great I AM who is the beginning and ending of all things, has something He longs to do on your behalf to restore you *fully* to the wholeness He envisioned for you when He made you?

Do you have an understanding of the ways in which God wants you to become His agent on this earth?

Listen.

And listen again.

Listen today.

CHAPTER SEVEN

Be Like Jesus

That's the only way to be authentically yourself AND be fully effective.

Jesus came into Galilee, *preaching* the gospel of the kingdom of God.... And he *preached* in their synagogues throughout all Galilee, and cast out devils.

—MARK 1:14, 39, ITALICS ADDED FOR EMPHASIS

And he began again to *teach* by the sea side: and there was gathered unto him a great multitude....
And he *taught* them many things by parables.

—MARK 4:1–2, ITALICS ADDED FOR EMPHASIS

And whithersoever he entered, into villages, or cities, or country, they laid the sick in the streets, and besought him that they might touch if it were but the border of his garment: and as many as touched him were *made whole.*

—MARK 6:56, ITALICS ADDED FOR EMPHASIS

You might assume that once I had heard from God, I was off and running in an ever-effective and growing *healing* ministry, with many souls saved and many mighty miracles such as the ones I had seen and personally experienced in Brother Moncey's tent.

You might assume that I began to hear God's voice regularly, or at least often.

That was not the case.

Within two months after I was healed, I became involved in full-time ministry—doing the work of a pastor at times and the work of an evangelist at times—but I make no claim to having had a genuine anointing of God to heal the sick for more than a decade. I felt I had an anointing of God for healing at *times*, but not very long at a time. Assuredly, I did not have enough of that anointing to overcome my fears of facing the sick and demon-possessed.

Even so, I knew that God not only could heal, but that He desired to heal. One incident stands out vividly in my memory.

While I was pastoring the Pentecostal Holiness Church in Toccoa, Georgia, one of our deacons, Clyde Lawson, had an accident and called me to come pray for him. Clyde was a mechanic and he had been working on a car when he dropped a heavy motor on his foot. The toes of that foot had been crushed and he was bleeding, and in great pain. When my associate, Bill Lee, and I arrived on the scene, Clyde was crying out in such pain that he could not even talk. All he could do was point at his crushed foot in a way that signaled he wanted our prayers.

Feelings of compassion came over me and without thinking I knelt down and touched the end of his shoe with my hand. I said a few words of earnest prayer and stood up. The moment I straightened up, Clyde Lawson quit screaming. He tried to move his toes in his shoe and found that he could. The pain was gone. The bleeding had stopped. He jumped to his feet, stomped his foot on the floor of his garage, and said, "Brother Roberts, what did you do to me?"

I said, "I didn't do a thing."

He said, "Yes, you did. The pain is gone. My foot is healed."

I was as amazed as he was. He tore off his shoe and showed us his foot. His toes were perfectly normal.

Bill said to me as we drove away, "Brother Roberts, do you have that kind of power all the time?"

I said, "Bill, I wish I did."

He said, "If you had that kind of power all the time, you could bring a revival to this world."

I didn't have any doubt about that. I just didn't have any clue as to how a person might develop that kind of power *all the time.*

Unless you have been a young Pentecostal preacher ministering mostly to rural people who had lived simple lives and liked a religious routine that was highly predictable, you may not be able to understand what my life as a preacher was like in the 1930s and 1940s.

As a young man just starting out, I wanted the favor of my elders and the acceptance of the people in my religious denomination. I longed for more of God's power, but I had no role models for how to experience that power, and no role models for how to use such power wisely. I patterned my style of preaching after the leaders in my church world, and I conducted my services according to the patterns the "older saints" had established.

Some of this need for approval and acceptance was a carryover from my childhood and teenage years.

If there was ever a boy who wanted to be LIKE other people so he could be LIKED by other people, it was Oral Roberts as a child.

I have an old photo in my home that tells a lot. Vaden and I are about twelve and ten years old, respectively. Vaden is wearing a white shirt and neatly ironed slacks, a bowtie at his neck, his hair slicked back, and taking on the camera with a confident smile. I am standing next to him in overalls and crumpled shirt, barefoot, my head down, and obviously sending a message of awkwardness, shyness, and a desire to be anywhere but there having my photograph taken.

That photo is indicative of my life as a boy. I felt unwelcome at most family events, even though in reality I may have been completely welcome. I felt unworthy to open my mouth—I never knew if any sound would come out. I felt embarrassed at my gangliness as a growing boy—who eventually grew to be taller than my father and siblings. I withdrew whenever I didn't know the proper thing to do or what might be expected of me for me to receive approval and inclusion. I *wanted desperately* to be like the other guys and eventually, to be praised as highly as Vaden and others in my family.

That early lack of self-worth disappeared to a great extent when I won the heart of the lovely Miss Lutman who consented to become my "darling wife Evelyn." Evelyn was willing to leave the "sure deal" of a teacher's career and launch out with me into an ever-moving, always-changing life of ministry, many times not knowing where she would be living the next month or how much money she would have to prepare meals and buy diapers and clothes for our babies. No man could ever ask for a more loving and faithful wife. Evelyn believed in me when I didn't believe in myself. She had a profound effect on me all of our life together, and although she's now been in heaven for several years, the memory of her still guides me in many ways. I know just what she would say and can almost hear her voice at times, speaking to me in calm but measured words just what she believes I need to hear about who I am and how God values me.

Even with Evelyn by my side, however, I still had residual effects from those early years. I *wanted* to be a success among my peers and have the respect and admiration of my elders.

The conflict between what I wanted, and what was...

The discrepancy between what I believed, and what others wanted...

The chasm between what God was saying, and what I was experiencing...

Grew.

On the one hand, I was excited about taking God's healing power to my generation and freeing suffering people from the shackles the devil had put on their lives—and was eager to do so, but instead, I found myself preaching doctrine and trying to appease the small group of people in any congregation who seemed to have control over what should be preached, how the church should be run, how much the pastor should be paid or not paid, and what kind of balance should be struck between a minister's work as a pastor and as an evangelist.

In many ways, I was unhappy during most of the first twelve years I worked as a minister within the church world, but that feeling of frustration and being unsettled in my spirit escalated when I moved back to my home state to continue my education.

A Command that Could Not Be Sidestepped

It was not long after Clyde Lawson's foot was healed that we left Toccoa and moved to central Oklahoma where I enrolled in Oklahoma Baptist University at Shawnee, Oklahoma. Evelyn and I had a daughter named Rebecca and a son named Ronald, whom we called Ronnie. I went to school during the week and preached revival meetings on the weekends, often hitchhiking to meetings as far away as a hundred miles.

About a year later, I was called to be the pastor of the church at Enid, Oklahoma, and there, I enrolled at Phillips University. Not long after, I began to teach one day a week at Southwestern College in nearby Oklahoma City. My life was full to the brim with family, ministry, studying, and teaching responsibilities.

Some of the best people in the world were members of that Enid church and they loved me as if I was their son. I had a wonderful ministry among them and in the first eleven months, about fifty

new people joined the church. It seemed as if this was going to be the place of my best ministry for a very long time.

And then, I began to hear echoes of what God had said to me twelve years before on my way to Brother Moncey's tent: "Son, I am going to heal you and you are to take My healing power to your generation."

I'd be sitting in a classroom and I would hear God say, "Son, I am going to heal you and you are to take My healing power to your generation."

I'd be studying my Bible as I prepared a sermon, and I'd hear God say, "Son, I am going to heal you and you are to take My healing power to your generation."

I'd drive up to my church office on a weekday and I'd hear God say, "Son, I am going to heal you and you are to take My healing power to your generation."

I could not escape His command.

God did not speak to me in the same profound silence or with the same intensity of voice on these occasions; it was more as if I was suddenly forced to recall and to relive that incident from the past.

Many people seem to be able to relate to what I experienced. Something comes to mind again, and again, and yet again. In recalling an incident from the past, the person seems to "relive" the moment—feeling the same feelings, having the same response, hearing the same sounds, and sometimes even smelling the same aromas or feeling the same sensations.

There was a profound chasm between what I believed *could* happen in a setting in which God's power was fully manifested, and what *was* happening in the daily routine of my life.

I felt increasingly that going to church just for the sake of going to church was about the dullest thing a person could do. When the anointing of God is not upon the pastor or the people, and His presence is not experienced, there isn't very much of interest to the soul of man. Even as the pastor, sitting on the platform about to preach, I often wished I was somewhere else on a Sunday morning.

Again, let me reinforce that the people in my church loved me, but as I told them about the great miracles of Bible days and shared with them the great hunger in my heart to see that kind of miracle-working power at work in the world in our day, my messages seemed ineffective, at least from my perspective. The people would give me a decent hearing and then get up and go home. They seemed more concerned with their wheat crops, their jobs, their in-laws, and the common problems of life than they were with seeking God for more of His great power. They were loyal to the church, paid their tithes, came to the services, and lived good lives. But that was about the sum total of their religion. I didn't have enough power to change their believing, and they didn't long for that power for themselves.

I also came to the realization one day that sick people didn't come to church. They tended to stay at home. And furthermore, nobody in the church was willing to admit to any problems. They dressed in their finest, put on their happiest faces, and one could only guess at the problems that were keeping them awake at night or tearing at the fabric of their marriages, families, and inner selves.

The church people were there but didn't care much about healing. The sick who cared about getting well weren't there. I felt a tug-of-war deep in my spirit.

Then the day came in May of 1947 when I was sitting in a classroom and struggling to stay quiet and stay seated as a sociology professor droned on and on about how God could not *possibly* have made Eve from a rib taken from Adam's side. I was totally repulsed by his lecture. Who is any finite mortal being to tell others what God *cannot* do!

All of the frustration and desires that had been brewing and mingling in me for years suddenly rose up and I did something very

uncharacteristic for me at that time. I stood up, excused myself, and walked out of that classroom. As I walked out of the building into the bright Oklahoma sunshine, God spoke:

> "Son, do not be like other men. Do not be like your denomination. Do not be like other ministers. Be like Jesus, and heal the people as He did."

I knew His voice. I felt a thrill throughout my being at hearing Him again call me "Son." I knew His words to me were a life-altering command.

God had spoken directly to me once again.

The time had come to make some hard choices.

A Willingness to Obey... but How?

I immediately began to question, "But how, God?" The answer came:

> "Read the four gospels and the book of Acts on your knees, three times within thirty days, and I will show you how to be like Jesus."

With eager anticipation, I began to do what God had told me to do!

I could hardly wait to discover what God had for me to learn. I was desperate for more of His power. I longed to be like Jesus. I longed to see the people healed. I knew the key had been given to me for unlocking the door into my future.

Now, I certainly had read the Bible through a number of times at that point—in fact, I once calculated that I had probably read the New Testament through more than one hundred times when God spoke to me to read the four gospels and the book of Acts on my knees, three times in thirty days. I began to read again, however, with new intensity, as if I had never read this part of the Bible before. I would go to my bedroom, close the door, get down on my knees by the bed, spread my Bible out before me, and start reading. I would read that way until my knees were so cramped I could scarcely stand up.

The most amazing and marvelous thing happened.

I saw and understood Jesus as I had never seen or understood Him before. He seemed to rise up from the pages of my open Bible. I don't know whether I had a series of God-imparted *visions* or my God-given ability to *envision* was enhanced, but either way, I *saw* Jesus in three dimensions, moving about the countryside of Israel, and doing His work as a preacher, teacher, and miracle-working healer. There He was before me, not only willing but eager for me to see Him in the fullness of both His humanity and divinity.

I saw Jesus as a man of power, yet a man of deep compassion.

I saw Him as a man of action.

I saw Him as a simple man without any complications.

I saw that He came against life-limiting suggestions and life-shortening ailments with life-saving power.

I saw that He had no tolerance for and came strongly against four great enemies of mankind: sin, demons, disease, and fear.

I saw Jesus was a man's man, strong in body, strong in soul and mind, full of love and tenderness.

I saw that He spent two-thirds of His time healing the sick. In fact, I saw that Jesus had a three-fold ministry. He preached...He taught...and He healed. The three worked together.

- To preach is to proclaim the good news that God wants to have an intimate relationship with every person. To preach is to tell the plan of salvation and God's desire to meet every need in a person's life.

- To teach is to tell others what the Bible says about the way men and women are to live in right relationship with

God. Teaching involves explaining the lasting principles and concepts of God—His nature, His commands, and His promises.

- To heal is to remedy whatever might be lacking or faulty in a person's *life—whatever* is not in keeping with God's original creation and design. It is doing whatever you see to do to help another person be made whole.

Finally, I came to the quick conclusion that what Jesus did, He not only wanted but authorized His disciples to do. He expected His disciples to have the same faith and compassion for the deliverance of lost and suffering humanity as He had. He transmitted His power to them and gave them full authority to cast out devils, heal the sick, preach the gospel, win souls, and inspire people to believe for the full blessings of God in their lives.

Jesus wasn't about religion. He was about relationship.

He wasn't about protocol. He was about powerful persuasion.

He wasn't about compromise. He was about change.

He wasn't seeking fame or fortune. He was seeking souls for heaven.

As I moved into reading the book of Acts, I saw that the followers of Jesus, filled with the Holy Spirit that Jesus had sent to them, conducted their lives as if Jesus was still present with them and working through them. The spirit within them was *His* Spirit!

I saw that the apostles of Jesus had the power to heal, to work miracles, and to cast out demons. Miracles were not a rarity in places where the apostles preached, taught, and healed—miracles were the norm!

I didn't believe for one second that the days of great miracles, signs, and wonders were over. I had a conversation with Papa one afternoon about this. We were sitting in two cane-bottomed chairs that we had leaned up against the back of the house where I was living. I said, "Papa, why don't preachers heal the sick like they did in Bible times?"

He said, "I don't know."

I said, "Well, Papa, don't we have the same commission to heal the sick in our day as the Lord gave His disciples back then?"

He said, "Yes, I believe we are supposed to do just like they did back then."

I said, "Papa, do you believe that before Jesus comes He will pour out another great healing revival such as they had in the days of the early church?"

He said, "Oral, I have believed for thirty years that before Jesus comes there will be a worldwide revival. I believe it now stronger than ever. I believe God will raise up men and give them power to raise the dead, to heal blind eyes, to cast out devils, and when that is done, I believe Jesus will come."

I believed what Papa said and reading the four gospels and the book of Acts three times in thirty days only deepened my belief. But what was I to do?

I did not know *how* to move forward, but I was determined to find out *how*. I fasted and prayed, and God revealed some amazing things to me from His Word. I became even more determined to discover more. I knew I was on the verge of something big, and something important. I intended to have God's power whatever the cost.

What God's Words to Me Mean to Your Life Today

God has different work for every person to do but I am thoroughly convinced of this: God has a "Jesus way" for you to live and for you to accomplish your purpose in life.

1. Be like Jesus.

That is a word that the Lord desires to speak into every person's heart. *Every* Christian needs to make "being like Jesus" his or her goal.

Frankly, I don't see many Christians who make "being like Jesus" their top priority. In many ways, countless millions upon millions of people in this world are just as I was: They are trying to be *like* other people, in order to be *liked* by other people. Some pattern their clothing styles, their hairstyles, other areas of "fashion," and even their lifestyles after the people they see in magazines, on television, in music videos, and in the movies. Some seek out role models in the worlds of business, politics, academia, or a particular profession and say, "I want to be just like that person." Some seek to copy a particular preacher.

While I believe it is entirely acceptable to learn what a person can learn from somebody who has good character, good knowledge, and the power of God in their lives, God's challenge to us is not to be a carbon copy of any other person—but rather, to be like Jesus.

We are to have Christ's character.

Jesus was overflowing with what we in the church world call the "fruit of the Spirit": love, joy, peace, patience, gentleness, goodness, faith, meekness, self-control. (SEE GALATIANS 5:22–23.) We are to be like Jesus in our motivations, our desires, and our character traits.

We are to have Christ's mind.

The apostle Paul wrote to the first-century Christians, "Let this mind be in you, which was also in Christ Jesus" (PHILIPPIANS 2:5). He wrote to the church at Rome: "Be not conformed to this world: but be ye transformed by the renewing of your mind, that ye may prove what is that good, and acceptable, and perfect, will of God" (ROMANS 12:2).

We are to have Christ's compassion.

The Gospels tell us that when Jesus looked out over the sea of humanity, He was "moved with compassion" in two ways: He was moved with compassion because the people were without God, and

He was moved with compassion because the people were sick and in many cases, outcasts from their families, church world, and society. (SEE MATTHEW 9:36 AND MARK 1:41.) We are to have compassion for people in those same ways.

We are to say what Jesus said and do what Jesus did.

Jesus gave His followers full authority to continue His ministry. In fact, He *commissioned* them in these ways:

- "All power is given unto me in heaven and in earth. Go ye therefore, and teach all nations, baptizing them in the name of the Father, and of the Son, and of the Holy Ghost: Teaching them to observe all things whatsoever I have commanded you: and, lo, I am with you always, even unto the end of the world" (MATTHEW 28:18–20).

- "Go ye into all the world, and preach the gospel to every creature. He that believeth and is baptized shall be saved; but he that believeth not shall be damned. And these signs shall follow them that believe; In my name shall they cast out devils; they shall speak with new tongues; They shall take up serpents"—indicative of every evil thing—"and if they drink any deadly thing, it shall not hurt them; they shall lay hands on the sick, and they shall recover" (MARK 16:15–18).

These words of Jesus were not only to those who might become members of the professional clergy. They were words of *command* to all the followers of Christ, not only in the days immediately following Christ's death, resurrection, and ascension, but to Christian believers throughout the ages.

What tremendous faith and confidence Jesus had in His followers!

If you are a person who struggles with having a low opinion of your own worth and value before God, or low value in the

eyes of other people, it is extremely vital that you hear the truth about yourself and Jesus from God: God calls you to become like Jesus, and He believes you *can* become like Jesus. He sees in you the potential for having the character, mind—which includes your abilities to perceive, understand, and apply information—and compassion of Christ. He empowers you by the Holy Spirit to say and do what Jesus would say and do if He were walking in your shoes, in your world, meeting the people you meet.

Don't listen to the way other people might define you.

Listen to the way God defines you.

Don't limit yourself to what other people tell you is your potential.

Listen to what God says.

Don't seek to become like the world or live according to the world's patterns of success.

Listen to what God calls you to be.

2. Get a strong picture of how Jesus would live in your world.

The Bible is available to you, too. Find a version that you enjoy reading and then read it. Ask God to show you Jesus in a new way.

Jesus calls you to have a three-fold ministry in your world, in your career—whether you are a professional minister of some type or a person sitting in the pew. He wants you to be willing and courageous in these areas:

- **Preaching**. This is simply telling others about Jesus and what He has done for you and others by His death on the cross and His resurrection from the dead.

- **Teaching**. You don't need to be a Bible scholar. You can tell others what you know to be God's truth. Start with your children or grandchildren, and your nieces and nephews.

- **Healing**. Begin to pray for others and expect a miracle. The more you pray for others, the more God will show you how to pray. The more you speak God's healing into the lives of others, the more you will understand how to do it.

God wants you and every Christian to be faithful in doing these things—in your own way, according to your own gifts from God, and in your families, social circles, communities, churches, and workplaces.

Ask God to show you *how* to be like Jesus in your world.

Evaluate Your Own Heart

Are you patterning your life after Jesus today?

Are you believing for all that you might be in Christ Jesus?

Do you have a good understanding of the way Jesus would live out His life if He was walking in your shoes?

Listen.

And listen again.

Listen today.

CHAPTER EIGHT

God's Method for Your Effectiveness

God has already prepared a WAY for you to succeed in what He has purposed for you to accomplish.

Behold, as the clay is in the potter's hand,
so are ye in mine hand.
—JEREMIAH 18:6

It is a merciful God who clouds the future and puts His hand over tomorrow. Had I been able to look down the road and see all the persecutions, criticisms, false accusations, and hardships that I was to face, I might have made another kind of decision, but God in His mercy let me see only from day to day.

Soon after God led me to the Bible and commanded me to be like Jesus, God began to deal with me in a manner I had never experienced before. I began to have recurring vivid dreams in which I saw masses of people stream past me, and I saw that every one of them was sick in some way. Even those who didn't look sick on the outside were people I knew in the wisdom of my dream were sick. God seemed to be showing me that *every person is sick in some way*—a truth that I have come to understand far more clearly through the years. Truly, *every* person has *some* need for healing.

One night I awakened from a deep sleep to find myself in our back yard under our pear tree. When I came to myself I was sobbing and praying. In my entire life up to that point, I had never walked in my sleep, and when I discovered that I was in the back yard I felt strange. But I went back into the house and crawled into bed and didn't say anything to my wife Evelyn. This happened to me several times, until one night I found myself in the corner of the bathroom on my knees and sobbing. As I came to myself I looked up and saw Evelyn standing by me. She touched me on the shoulder and said, "Oral, what in the world are you doing?"

I answered truthfully, "Evelyn, I don't know."

She took me by the arm and led me back into the bedroom where we sat down on the side of the bed.

She said, "Oral, what's the matter with you?"

I said, "Evelyn, I don't know."

She said, "Yes, you do, Oral."

When she said those words, it was as if a light turned on in my mind. I said, "Yes, Evelyn, I do know. I haven't known until this minute, but now I know. My time to heal the sick has come and I don't have the power of God to do it."

I told her what God had said to me in the back of a borrowed car on the night that I was healed of tuberculosis. In the twelve years since that first time God spoke to me, I had not told anyone about hearing God's voice or His command for me to take His healing power to my generation. Evelyn listened and then said, "Oral, I knew it. I've known that this was coming for a long time."

I said, "You knew it?"

She said, "Yes, Oral, I knew it."

I said, "Who told you?"

She said, "Nobody told me, Oral. I just knew it."

I said, "Evelyn, I don't know what to do."

She said, "Yes, you do."

I certainly didn't know what to do about launching a ministry of healing but I did know the first step to take in finding out. I said to her, "Don't cook me any meals until I tell you." I began to fast and pray.

I had never read any books on fasting or heard any teaching about it, so I really didn't know how to fast. On a few occasions through the years, I had "fasted" from a meal and prayed instead. That was about the extent of my personal experience with fasting. As I look back on it now, I'm happy that I did not know how to fast, for I fasted from my heart and not after a particular method. God looks on the heart of a man and deals with him accordingly.

During my fasting I would spend the same time in prayer as it would normally take me to eat a meal. In other words, when a mealtime came I figured out about how many minutes it would normally have taken me to eat that meal, and I would spend that amount of time in prayer. At times I read the Bible as part of my prayer time, at other times I just prayed.

The net result was that I was eating just enough to maintain the ability to do my job, and I increased my prayer life considerably. My attention seemed to be focused continually on Jesus. My heart burned more and more to be like Him. Over and over I beseeched God for His strength, both for body and soul. I knew and believed the verse of Scripture that says, "God's strength shall be made perfect in weakness." (SEE 2 CORINTHIANS 12:9.)

Fasting was not easy for me. I felt great weakness in my body. Even so, I refused to let anyone or anything deter me from what I was doing. I lost thirty-two pounds in a very short period of time, and while I did everything in my power to keep my fasting a secret, it's difficult to keep a secret when you are losing weight rapidly. People began to give me all sorts of advice, but I had no interest in what people said. I only wanted the Lord to impart to me what He wanted for my life.

I finally felt that I had reached a point of no return. I was desperate for the fullness of God's power in my life. I made a decision to have it out with God—a showdown of sorts. I went to my study in the Enid Pentecostal Holiness Church where I was the pastor. I locked the door and stood before God, talking to Him from the depths of my heart. I felt I was closer to Him than to any human being. For the past several weeks I had actually spent more time in His presence than I had with my family. I said, "Lord, I have made up my mind. I have reached the place in my thinking from which there is no return. This is it, Lord. I have been asking You for many months for Your power. I have earnestly prayed for Your power. You told me twelve years ago I was to take Your healing power to my generation and I cannot do that without Your anointing. Today is the end of my searching. I am going to find Your answer. I am going to lie down on this floor before You and I will not rise until You speak to me."

I once read that psychologists have determined that when a person truly makes up his or her mind, that person's mind can no longer be swayed. Mine was made up. When I told God I would not rise from the floor until He had revealed Himself to me, I meant every word of it. I moved the chairs back, stretched out on the floor with my face down, and began to pray. It was not a prayer in which I told God what I thought He should do. Rather, it was a begging prayer for Him to give me more of Himself. I prayed from the heart. As I lay there I felt like a tiny speck in His vast universe. I was one man striving with the Almighty. I poured my soul out to Him like water from a great jar.

I have no idea how long I lay on the floor praying. I never looked at a clock. Time really didn't matter. But the more I prayed, the more I knew that somehow in a mysterious and indescribable way, the old Oral Roberts was beginning to fade. A strange power seemed to take control of my mind and heart and I knew I was praying, but I could not distinguish all of my own words.

Somewhere in that prayer I lost contact with the physical and made contact with the spiritual. The last memory I have until later was that I suddenly had a feeling of release—that my struggling and striving were over. I felt God was with me and I was with God. Had someone come into my pastor's study at that moment, they probably would have thought I was dead. There was no moving of my physical body, only the wild beating of my heart. I felt something going out of me and something coming into me. All of this may have taken several hours. I truly don't know. It *seemed* like only a moment.

And then God spoke to me. His words were like those of a military commander, clear and crisp. He said:

"Get on your feet."

Slowly, I got up, facing the door. I started swaying but caught myself by holding onto the wall. As I stood there feeling a little dizzy, He said:

"Go get in your car."

As I went down the center aisle of the church I was swaying so much I had to catch the ends of the pews on either side to keep myself from falling. I slipped in behind the steering wheel of my car and sat there with my hands at my side. God said:

"Drive one block and turn right."

I closed the door of the car, started the engine, drove one block, and as I made a right-hand turn, the Lord said:

> "From this hour you will heal the sick and cast out devils by My power."

It seemed as if ten thousand volts of electricity surged through my body and that a thousand pounds were lifted from my shoulders. My head cleared completely, my voice became vibrant, my body trembled, and I let out a huge sigh that I shall always remember. I drove straight to the parsonage, 8065 West Randolph Street, Enid, Oklahoma, and shouted, "Evelyn, cook me a meal! The Lord has spoken to me!" She knew immediately that God had revealed Himself to me, for she saw it in my face.

The Battle Began

When a man receives a specific anointing from God, the battle has just begun. I began to make plans for a major healing service. My first plan was to have two or three regular services in the church devoted to healing. Some of the brethren, however, thought I should hold a larger healing service outside of Enid, where I was not known. I told them, "No, I'm going to hold it in Enid where everybody knows me and where it will be the hardest." I felt if I could have a successful healing service there, I could have it anywhere.

Finally, we decided to secure a downtown auditorium and we announced one service open to everybody in the city and surrounding area. We scheduled the meeting for a Sunday afternoon at two o'clock. Personally, I was staking everything on that service.

I told God that He would need to supply three things for me to have a confirmation that I was doing what He wanted me to do. That's a somewhat dangerous position to take, but I had strong evidence from the story of Gideon in the Bible that God will provide confirmation for us that we are doing His will. (SEE JUDGES 6–7.) First, I wanted one thousand people at the service. Second, I wanted the offering to cover the expense of renting the auditorium and arranging for the sound system, and so forth—without any pleading on the part of any person. Third, I wanted at least one person to be healed in a way that the person knew it and I knew it.

I told God that if He did not answer those three requests, I would resign my church pastorate, return my ordination papers to my denominational conference, stop being a minister, and return to private life. I went so far as to go to a downtown clothing store and ask the owner if he might have an opening in the near future. When he said he might have an opening, I decided that if worst came to worst I would ask for a job in his store to support my family.

These were desperate things to say to God and I certainly do not recommend such vows to anybody else. They were vows only for me, but they may give you a hint as to how committed I was and how dependent upon God I felt.

When I got to the auditorium that afternoon, I went in a side door so I could move directly to the platform. I asked the caretaker of the building, "How many people are out in the audience?" He said, "Twelve hundred people are already seated."

Later, before I preached, an offering was received. Someone announced in just a few words that the offering was only to pay the rental for the auditorium and related expenses, a prayer was said, and the offering was collected. After the men counted it they brought me a slip of paper on which they had written the amount of the offering: "$163.03." That was $3.03 above what we needed.

I began to preach, and I had not preached for more than ten minutes when the anointing power of God struck my mortal flesh. I began to tingle from the crown of my head to the soles of my feet. My brain was clear and sharp, the words rolled out of my mouth, and I heard myself preaching as I had never preached before. I had titled my sermon, "If You Need Healing—Do These Things." It was a message about how people might turn their faith loose for a healing miracle.

I only made it about halfway through that sermon when the power of God became so great inside me that I could not stand still. I leaped off the high platform down to the lower floor and when I did, the audience immediately leaped to its feet as if by a prearranged signal. About two or three hundred people began to come down the aisles toward me. People began shouting and rejoicing. Some were weeping. I don't know how the "healing line" took shape, but suddenly there was a long line of people coming to me, single file, and I began to lay my hands on them one by one.

When I laid my hands on an elderly German woman who had had a stiff hand for thirty-eight years, she suddenly screamed at the top of her voice that she was healed. She raised her hand high and began to open and close it to show the people how God had removed the stiffness and given her the ability to use her hand for the first time in almost four decades. Those close by her saw the physical evidence of this healing, even as I did, and this greatly increased their faith for their own healing miracles. I prayed for people until six o'clock that evening.

When the service was over, my clothes were wet from perspiration, my hair was disheveled, and my body was tired, but I still felt strong as a lion inside. There was a fire burning in my soul. God had confirmed His word to me. I had started in a place where it was hardest to start. I felt suddenly as if the whole world was waiting for me, and I knew that as soon as I could secure my release from teaching at the university and help the church find a new pastor, I would take God's anointing to wherever He led me.

An Ongoing Sign of God's Anointing

After I resigned from the pastorate in Enid, Evelyn and I went to Tulsa, Oklahoma, where I conducted a nine-week revival and healing crusade. I hadn't planned for it to last that long, but God had moved in powerful ways and it became very obvious that Tulsa was to be the place for our ministry office and our home.

Shortly after finishing the nine-week crusade in Tulsa, I conducted a one-night service in Nowata, Oklahoma, a small city about fifty miles to the north. I preached to an overflow crowd of three hundred in a small church sanctuary, but there was such a spirit of expectancy in that crowd that when I made the appeal to the unsaved to accept Christ, there wasn't enough room at the front of the building for them to stand. As became my practice for the remainder of my healing ministry, I prayed for those in the aisles and throughout the building who wanted to accept Jesus Christ of Nazareth as their Savior, and *then* I began the healing line.

A mother brought her young son, who was totally deaf, into the prayer line. As I stood there looking at this mother and then at her son, who appeared to be about eight years old, God suddenly spoke to me:

> "Son, you have been faithful to this hour and now you will feel My presence in your right hand. Through My presence, you will be able to detect the presence of demons. You will know their number and name, and will have My power to cast them out."

God's words were distinct and clear. His power surged into my right hand immediately. And given the situation standing immediately before me, I instinctively placed the first finger of each hand into the little boy's ears. I felt nothing of God's presence in my left hand—it was merely flesh touching flesh. My right hand, however, was strong, warm, and had power surging through it. I find it difficult to explain this sensation. It is like an electrical charge, only without any stinging or hurting, and it extends from

my elbow down through my fingertips. I took my fingers out of the boy's ears and looked at my hands. They looked the same.

I put the finger of my right hand back into one ear of that little boy and I said, "In the name of Jesus Christ of Nazareth, you tormenting spirit of deafness, come out! Come out!"

Instantly, the little fellow looked around. He put his hands over his ears, and he began to cry and look at his mother.

I said to her, "He is apparently hearing noises, and it scares him." I asked her to speak to her son. She called his name and he answered. I asked her to stand behind him, where he couldn't see her lips, and talk to him in a normal voice. She did. Each time she spoke, he whirled around to her and echoed her words back to her as best he could. He had some capacity of speech but it was not very clear.

The audience and I were all in awe. Someone pushed a woman in the healing line toward me. She was sitting in a kitchen chair to which wheels had been attached. She had used that chair to scoot around for eight years. My right hand flew to her forehead. I felt the presence of God race down my arm and into my hand and into her being. She leaped up out of her chair, raised her legs up and down a few times, looked around, and then took off running through the crowd, praising God and crying.

The people in the crowd then began to praise God, shouting and dancing in the aisles in what I can only describe as divine ecstasy. I was just as astonished and thrilled as they were. It was totally unlike anything I had ever experienced before.

Now, I had *felt* God's presence, but it had been a flow of His power that was throughout my entire being. I knew a number of Holy Spirit-filled people who had experienced this, something the people in my denomination called "feeling the power of God." This time, however, God's presence was specifically directed to my right hand. It was as if my lower arm and hand became a "tool" that God had claimed for His use.

Dealing with Demons

In seeking more of God's power, I had focused my desire on God's *healing* power, primarily for physical disease. God's words to me about detecting and commanding demons was something I had not anticipated.

I did believe this and continue to believe this about the devil's power and sickness: The devil seeks to oppress all people and sickness is an oppression. Physical illness is many times inextricably linked to a "spirit" of illness. This is *not* to say, however, that all sickness is a sign of demonic possession.

Oppression, yes.

Possession, not often.

There are times when demonic possession produces sickness in a person, and there are certain mental or emotional illnesses that seem to open a person to demonic possession. But, I never assumed as I approached the healing lines that I was about to battle demonic possession. It was always something of a surprise to me when I encountered the presence of demons in control of a person—and I will quickly add this—the controlling demons seemed generally more surprised at encountering me!

Demons are very real entities of evil. I am very aware that many people today don't believe demons exist. Jesus acknowledged their reality. The first apostles acknowledged their reality. I have encountered them face to face. I have no doubt they are real.

Demons are foul. They attempt to strip a person of his or her humanity, often causing people to exhibit animal or reptile behaviors—darting eyes, flickering tongues, growling noises, and so forth. They emit a terrible odor. They sometimes twist and contort a person's face or body, and they sometimes give people unusually great strength. They often cause a person's voice to have a strange, eerie quality to it.

Demons seek embodiment in human beings so they might engage in evil. They can cause terrible things to happen either to the person or through the person.

But let me quickly assure you, no demon can resist a Holy Spirit command to come out of a person the demon is afflicting.

I must also add this: Not every person who is controlled by demons will allow himself to be taken into the presence of a person who has been anointed by God for their deliverance. But, on numerous occasions when people with demons stood before me in the healing line, even the demons seemed shocked that I knew they were present, I knew their number, and I knew their general name.

There are no fancy formulas for casting demons out of a person. I simply commanded them to come out of the person they had been afflicting, tormenting, or manipulating. Demons are no more powerful than diseases—they both are subject to God's power in the same way. Demons, however, tend to leave a person immediately. Even in cases of demonic oppression, the "spirit" of illness can and often does leave immediately. Not every person is instantly healed of a physical ailment, but I do know this: While some physical healings occur over time, the healing *begins* in an instant. It is that "instant beginning" that is always the work of Almighty God.

Eventually, I found that I primarily was able to detect a demonic spirit in three ways: one, by the smell of a person's breath; two, by the unusual look in the person's eyes; and three, by the feeling in my right hand.

God's Power in My Right Hand

After the Nowata service I reflected on what had happened. I had more questions than answers. I certainly did not have a clear understanding immediately that what had happened in and through my hand was something that was going to remain with me. I considered the possibility that God's word to me had been only for that service in Nowata. I did not feel that sensation in my arm or hand in the days that followed, and although I admit to trying, I could not make my hand and arm feel that powerful surge of God's presence.

A few days after the Nowata service, I was asked to conduct a service in Faith Tabernacle, a well-known Tulsa church in the late 1940s. Again there was an overflow crowd and great expectancy.

Irma Morris and her sister Eve came to the service. Evelyn and I had known these two women for several years and considered them to be friends. Irma had been in and out of a sanatorium for tuberculosis but she didn't seem to be improving, and Eve brought her to the service for healing prayer.

As I preached that night, I noticed that God's presence had come into my right hand, and I definitely felt His presence in my hand as I approached Irma in the healing line. She was burning up with fever, and the TB smell was on her body. I recognized that smell clearly from my own experience and I felt a strong hatred for tuberculosis welling up within me. My right hand shot out to her forehead as I commanded the TB to loose her body and let her go free in the name of Jesus of Nazareth.

Her body seemed to jump at my touch and she asked, "Oh, Oral, what did you do to me?"

I said, "What do you mean, Irma?"

She said, "Your right hand! It felt on fire when it touched me." Tears began to roll down her cheeks and she said, "Something from your right hand is causing a warmth to go through my lungs. My lungs are opening up. I believe I am being healed!"

I looked at my right hand. It looked the same as it always looked. She was right, however. The *inside of my arm and hand* were charged with God's presence.

Back at home after the service, I told Evelyn about what had happened in Nowata and then again, that night. I had not said a word to her or anybody about this overwhelming and mysterious

phenomenon. Evelyn was always very levelheaded and practical, even though she was a deeply spiritual woman who was always open to whatever God might have for her. From the beginning, she was deeply appreciative of God's using me to heal the sick.

Evelyn said, "Do you suppose if you put your hand on my head, Oral, I could feel that power?"

I said, "I don't know, Evelyn. It comes when it comes. So far it's only as I have preached and touched some of the sick people in the healing line."

She said, "Touch me, please."

I touched her and did not feel a thing. Neither did she.

She said, "Well, maybe if you prayed for this thing that is wrong in my body, it would happen. I haven't wanted to tell you, but I've been suffering. Something is wrong inside me."

I said, "How long have you been suffering? Why didn't you tell me?"

She said, "I've had this for several weeks."

Immediately I began to feel the presence of God run down my lower arm into my hand. Evelyn was standing there before me and in that moment, it was as if she was not my wife, but someone in the healing line. I laid my right hand on her, with the vibration going through it, and commanded whatever was causing her suffering to leave her.

She immediately cried, "Oh, Oral, you are right! It is in your right hand. It is God!"

I said, "But what about the pain. Is it still there?"

She said, "Oh, no! It is totally gone."

Then Evelyn began to pray a prayer that is still etched deeply in my soul: "Dear Lord, we know this is not something Oral has of himself. I know him too well for him to claim it is his own power. It's Your presence, Lord Jesus. Help us to hold it precious and to give You praise for it."

From that day, we never doubted that God's anointing for healing and deliverance, and His words about His presence in my right hand, were *permanent* words to me. That surging power of God in my right hand has never left me. I can still feel it flowing down my arm and through my hand when I lay hands on people for their healing.

There are many things I didn't fully understand about God's healing power at that time—and for that matter, I don't fully understand His healing power today. I certainly anticipated that whenever I felt God's presence in my right hand, anybody I touched would be healed. That didn't happen, and it surprised me. I also couldn't understand why other people didn't seem to feel that presence in my hand at times when I felt it. Even so, God's presence in my right hand was a sign to a great number of sick people that God was present to heal. Some who felt the warmth in my right hand but weren't healed regarded it as a touch of God's love that drew them closer to God. Either way, God was at work and He alone is responsible for healing.

My part is to touch people and in faith, come against anything that is keeping them from wholeness.

God's part is to heal and make whole.

This presence of God surging through my lower arm and hand was and is a sovereign act of God. My right hand is a *tool* in His infinitely powerful right hand, used for His purposes. The only part I may have had was this: God said, "You have been faithful to this hour...."

What God's Words to Me Mean to Your Life Today

There are four things from these experiences in hearing God's voice that I believe are directly for you today.

1. God wants you to be an effective Christian.

Being effective means "getting the job done." To be effective you must come to the place where you deeply desire *all* that God has for you. You must be willing to be used in any way *God* chooses.

Being effective means doing what *God* wants done, and in the way *God* requires. Each of us must determine not only *what* it is we are to do, but *how and when* we are to act. This is not only true for us in the general direction of our life as a whole, but in our day-to-day living.

God will not call you to do things that waste your time and energy. He will not ask you to engage in any activity or relationship that draws you away from His central purpose for your life.

God wants you to be *effective* for Him and He will honor your desire to be effective.

Listen for God's words to you about the management of your time, your talents, your resources. Listen for Him to tell you what to do...and also what not to do. He will add some things, even as He may subtract others in order to prepare you for *maximum* effectiveness.

2. God calls you to obedience.

From my viewpoint, there is absolutely no logical reason for God to tell me to get up, go to my car, drive a block, and turn right. I have only two possible explanations for that: He was requiring my very specific, immediate, and practical obedience, or He was perhaps indicating to me that the flow of His power into my life was going to happen as I moved away from the role of being a pastor. His power did not come to me on the floor of my pastor's office. It came to me while I was on the road. As I look back over the years, for literally decades, I was "on the road" doing the work of an evangelist more than half of any given year.

God requires instant and full obedience from every person He uses in powerful ways. That's true for the great heroes of the Bible. It's true for the great men and women of God who are in ministry today.

God is not looking only for your general obedience to His overall plan for your life. He is looking for your willingness to obey Him in every decision, every choice, every hour.

God may very well ask you to leave what you know—the people, the place, the activity or job—and enter the realm of the unknown, where you will encounter new people, perhaps live and work in a new place, and engage in new activities that are increasingly fulfilling and meaningful to you.

When you hear God's command, be quick to obey.

3. God empowers what God commands.

For whatever God calls a person to do, He makes complete provision for His command to be fulfilled. The entire provision may not come up front, or be instantaneous, but the full provision is there to be accessed by faith over time. Furthermore, when God calls a person to undertake a particular challenge, He gives both the spiritual power and the courage for the person to *begin*. As in the case of provision, all the courage and spiritual authority necessary may not come in an instant deluge, but it will come—step by step, day by day.

Listen for God to give you words of assurance, confirmation, and encouragement.

4. God honors those who are faithful.

A pastor once said to me, "Oral, with God having you feel His presence in your right hand, and the tremendous response of the sick to it, where does that leave the rest of us ministers?"

I said, "I don't know. I had nothing to do with God doing this in my life. I do know that God doesn't deal with us all alike. Our goals as ministers are the same—to see lost souls saved and people delivered—but we are different people and God uses people in different ways. What each of us must do is be faithful in serving God as best we know how to be faithful. We must acknowledge that He is the Source of all spiritual power in our lives. We are not in charge. He is."

God honors those who are faithful.

He calls us to endure with persistence.

He rewards those who persevere.

Don't settle for anything less than God's full presence in your life. Hear His command to you today: Be faithful and be persistent in following the Lord.

Evaluate Your Own Heart

Are you willing to pursue God until He answers your deepest heart's cry?

Are you willing to obey God regardless of what He may call you to do?

Are you faithful in your walk with the Lord?

Do you feel desperate in your need for more of God's presence and power?

Listen.

And listen again.

Listen today.

CHAPTER NINE

Urgency and Increase

God always sets before us a challenge that is too big for us to achieve on our own.

The LORD spoke to Joshua, the son of Nun, Moses'
assistant, saying.… "No man shall be able to stand before
you all the days of your life; as I was with Moses,
so I will be with you. I will not leave you nor forsake you.
Be strong and of good courage.… Have I not commanded
you? Be strong and of good courage; do not be afraid,
nor be dismayed, for the LORD your God is with
you wherever you go."

—JOSHUA 1:1, 5–6, 9 NKJV

Prior to my first healing service, I had been like a racehorse waiting in the starting gate, ready and raring to burst forth with all the force and power it can exert. The healing service in Enid was the sounding of the gun that began my race. I came out of the gate and headed down the racetrack before me, going full speed ahead with only one thing in mind: to get to the finish line and God's winner's circle. The apostle Paul wrote, "Know ye not that they which run in a race run all, but one receiveth the prize? So run, that ye may obtain" (1 CORINTHIANS 9:24). I began running with a message of salvation, healing, and deliverance with all my heart, soul, mind, and strength.

My first healing service in Tulsa was held under Steve Pringle's tent in a driving rain with only a small crowd. But from the moment I opened my mouth, I was conscious of the anointing of the Holy Spirit. I was able to preach with the fire and the power of God upon me. A few sick people were present and we had a prayer line for them. Some of them felt they had been definitely and miraculously healed. Several others accepted Christ as their Savior. Within hours, the news of that service seemed to spread like wildfire across Tulsa. Three nights later, the thousand-seat tent was packed. On Sunday, the tent was filled and hundreds of people were standing around the edges.

I had only planned to preach for a week but at the end of that third service, Steve said, "Oral, you can't close this meeting. God is with you and you must stay another week." We continued the revival for nine straight weeks, with standing room only.

One of the things I noticed immediately was that my ministry seemed to be blotting out denominational barriers, color lines, and disunity. I concluded that just as desperately hungry people are willing to sit at a table with virtually anyone, so those who are desperately in need of God's healing and delivering power are willing to sit next to just about anybody under a tent.

I also knew almost immediately that the people were hungry for the news of *God's goodness and God's miracle-working power*. Nothing else really mattered because nothing else ignited their faith to believe for the miracles they needed in their lives. I threw my old sermon outlines away.

One night during this first healing crusade, a man none of us knew stood outside the tent for a few minutes, then pulled out a revolver, pointed it at me, and pulled the trigger. The bullet plowed through the canvas about eighteen inches above my head. The next day I saw the bullet hole. Standing there and hearing the shot but not really knowing what might happen next, I simply asked God to give me courage and divine protection until I had finished my work.

The news media headlined the shooting and overnight, my name was known nationwide as a man praying for the sick with miraculous results. The man later said in court that he didn't have any idea why he wanted to shoot at me. I saw his actions in light of God's words: "Ye thought evil against me: but God meant it unto good, to bring to pass, as it is this day, to save much people alive" (GENESIS 50:20).

Pastors in other states, upon hearing the news of my praying for the sick and the shot taken at me, began flying in to see what God was doing. I received invitations to come to their cities as soon as possible.

My ministry seemed to take off like a rocket.

As I began having larger crusades, not many auditoriums in America could handle the crowds. I recalled that I had been healed in a tent and that my first healing campaign was under a tent in Tulsa. I did not hear specifically from God in *words* that I was to buy a tent, but I did have a very powerful vision of my preaching in a big new tent.

I ordered a tent that could seat three thousand, as well as two trucks and semi-trailers to carry it, along with the folding chairs, piano, organ, and other equipment necessary for a major service. The first time we used the tent was June 1948 in Durham, North Carolina. The tent was jammed and we had to raise the tent flaps so thousands more could stand five and ten deep around the edges. By the last night of the crusade, twenty-one days later, the police estimated the crowd at nine thousand people. That figure was astonishing to me.

I began to preach that faith is something God has given to every person, and that God wants every person to release his faith to the Lord. I also recognized that it is helpful when people can touch something tangible as a "point of contact" for releasing their faith. I encouraged people to regard the instant my hand touched them as the pinpoint-targeted point at which they should send their faith to God. This teaching really caught hold among the people who came to my crusades and as more and more people caught hold of this concept, more and more healings occurred.

The crowds continued to grow. I traded in the three-thousand-seat tent for a bigger tent. Through the years, the tents grew larger and larger until eventually we had a tent that seated twelve thousand. It was the largest of its kind ever constructed, and it was designed to survive winds of up to a hundred miles an hour.

The larger the crowds grew, the greater the urgency in me to know that God's anointing was on my life and ministry. God seemed to be placing in front of me, month in and month out, audiences that were greater than those most other men of God were experiencing or had experienced, and with such diverse diseases and sins that the enormity and seriousness of the task before me was nearly overwhelming. More than any other person, I was aware of my humanness and shortcomings, and my inexperience in preaching and praying for thousands in a single meeting.

One thing I knew with certainty was that I could not, and would not, face a crowd without having several hours of rest and prayer before a service. I soon found that if I hung on expectantly in my preparation and prayers, the presence of God would start coming into my right hand before I went to the tent to preach. God's presence coming into my hand caused my faith to ignite inside me, and the awareness of His presence made me bolder in preaching and praying. It was no small thing for me to face thousands of needy and desperately ill people, many of whom were given no more hope by medical science. I made a vow to God that I would not preach or pray for the sick unless I had this sign of assurance that He was with me.

One night during my first crusade in Philadelphia, I had finished preparing as best I knew how and it dawned on me that I was not feeling the presence of God in my right hand. At first I panicked, thinking, *What if it doesn't come before my driver arrives? What about my vow to wait until I felt God's presence before facing the crowds? What would I do or say?*

I prayed, "Dear God! I have not been in this spot before. Please, will You help me?" My stomach was churning but I knew I had to be true to my vow. Over the next thirty minutes, I felt I might split apart. My driver arrived and I asked him to wait. I cried out to God, "Okay, God. I am Your property. You told me I was to take Your healing power to my generation. You know it was not my idea, and I did not call myself. I cannot go without absolutely knowing Your anointing is on me." I put down my Bible, took off my coat, sat down, and folded my hands in my lap. I said to the Lord, "I am going to sit here until You let me feel Your presence."

Ten minutes passed…twenty…I was still sitting there. I began to think about Bob DeWeese, my associate evangelist, and I knew that he was a spiritual and discerning man, a strong man, and we were very close in every way. I knew he would do what he had to do. And just as I was thinking that…the presence of God seized my right hand and began throbbing through it. I let out a yell, grabbed my Bible and coat, ran from the room, and hollered at my driver, "Let's go! God's presence is with me!" He drove as fast as he could to the great old Metropolitan Auditorium in the City of Brotherly Love.

Even before the car was fully stopped, I flung open the door and rushed toward the platform. The people in the crowd leaped to their feet and burst into tears and praise to God when they saw me. I didn't wait for Bob's complete introduction and we took no time singing "Where the Healing Waters Flow" as we usually did. I began to preach and then pray for the sick with such a powerful anointing

that I know, if stars fall at such times, they fell that night. Not all were healed, but there were many more healings than in any previous single service—literally thousands experienced healing of some type.

That service had a deep impact on my soul. I knew without any shadow of doubt that God was in total charge of what happened to me and through me. I also learned that God has His own timetable. Our schedules don't matter to God. Our obedience does.

Always, an Urgent Call to Expect More from God

Throughout the 1950s, God spoke to me a number of times, sometimes with messages just for me. Other messages were for the ministry as a whole—a ministry that seemed to have a constantly growing number of associates.

After my first healing revival, I received eight urgent letters from people who wanted me to pray and write back to them. Evelyn and I bought a little five-room house in Tulsa and I paid the previous owner twelve additional dollars for his small desk. There, at that desk, which we set up in the corner of our little dining room, I wrote to those eight people. Each week the number of letters grew. Three young women who attended the Tulsa crusade were secretaries at a large oil company. They told my wife Evelyn they'd be happy to come to our home directly after their jobs ended each day at 4:50 and help answer the mail. In the beginning they donated their time as each afternoon they would come to our home with their steno pads in hand, ready for me to dictate answers to the mail, which they then typed. They stayed right up to the start of the evening service. The hearts of these women were genuinely moved by seeing people saved and healed night after night, week after week. My heart was moved that they cared enough to help me in this practical way.

By the end of the summer of 1947 the mail was coming by sackloads. We turned our garage into an office and eventually, the entire house became our office and we moved into a larger house. One of the women who helped us with the mail, Ruth Hanson Rooks, stayed on with us as my secretary full-time, and through the decades, she has been the only secretary I have ever had. I can think of few people who have been more loyal or more professional than Ruth.

By the mid- to late 1950s, a decade after the start of the healing ministry, we were receiving a thousand letters a day. We had gone on radio and my weekly radio program was being carried by eight hundred radio stations by 1955. We were filming the crusades and airing them as black-and-white programs in prime-time slots. In addition to our radio programs, we were on two hundred television stations. In the 1950s we also established the Abundant Life Prayer Group, a dedicated group of men and women who worked eight-hour shifts, twenty-four hours a day, every day of the year, praying for the sick who called our headquarters from across the nation and around the world. In addition, some of my more popular sermons were edited into books. Reports of the crusades and testimonies of those who had been healed were reported in a monthly magazine titled *Healing Waters*, and later, *Abundant Life*. Selected messages were published in a quarterly devotional magazine titled *Daily Blessing*, which had a spiritual article for each day. By the 1960s, we were printing more than a million copies each month of the *Abundant Life* magazine and more than four hundred thousand copies of *Daily Blessing*. We were producing tracts and pamphlets in eighty-seven different languages—several million copies were circulated around the world.

All of these efforts, of course, meant a growing staff—including men who would transport the tent, as well as those who would arrange for the filming, photographing, and reporting of the crusades. Growing staff numbers required larger and larger facilities until by the end of the 1950s we were occupying a seven-story building near downtown Tulsa.

Those who were my associates in the ministry included a growing group of men and women whom I honored and recognized as my

"Partners for Deliverance." God showed me early in my ministry that I could not do on my own nearly as much as I could do if others would join in with me, not as mere "donors" or "offering givers," but as true Partners who would pray for the ministry, give regularly to the ministry, and tell others about our crusade meetings.

As I traveled with the big tents, I explained to those who came to my healing crusades that they each had a role they could take in our reaching the nation and eventually the world with the saving, healing, and delivering power of God.

On the one hand, the Partners did not have God's anointing on their lives to do what He had anointed me to do—to preach and pray. On the other hand, I did not have the resources they had, collectively, to take the tent to various locations or to travel overseas to speak in large arenas and auditoriums. Put our two hands together, however—almost as if we were shaking hands and sealing the deal—and we had a partnership that God would use and the devil could not stop.

The people quickly and eagerly caught the vision. One of my first Partners was my wife, Evelyn. She said, "Oral, I can't go every place where you are going to go, or attend every meeting God leads you to conduct. I have to stay home and raise our four children. But I can be your Partner for Deliverance. I can pray for you and when money comes directly into my hands, I can give to help send you. As your Partner, I will have a part in the reward that God will give in eternity for those whose souls are saved and whose lives have been changed by a healing miracle."

The truth is, I have never thought the healing ministry God gave to me was a one-man deal. The work was too big for one man. The burden was too great. The healing ministry God gave to me from the outset was *always* bigger than our financial resources at any given time, and always greater than anything we had ever sought to achieve or dreamed we could accomplish.

God reminded me of this again and again. Just when I'd think we were at the top of our game, He would speak. I heard from God a number of times in the 1950s. The messages were consistently urgent and spoke of increase.

He spoke to me as I was in hotel rooms during my preparation time for healing crusades:

> "It's later than you think."

And

> "You are to win one million souls during the next thirty-six months."

He spoke to me as I was driving along the Columbia River in Oregon in 1954:

> "My son, if you will believe, you can conceive a plan that will save millions."

In January of 1956, He spoke to me while I was in a hotel room in Hong Kong:

> "If you will seek My joy, My pleasure, and My faith, I will use you as an instrument to save ten million souls in the next ten years."

In 1959, as I sat alone in my house, He said:

> "You are to do three things immediately! First, you are to increase your overseas ministry. Second, you are to increase your emphasis upon the healing of the people. Third, you are to increase the number of your Partners immediately."

God's words propelled me forward. They built an even deeper sense of urgency, immediacy, and timeliness into me. They caused me to believe for even greater increase.

The more I acted on what God said, the more God held out new and higher goals before me.

What God's Words to Me Mean to Your Life Today

In these messages and in the many ways God confirmed them to my heart, I began to understand several things very clearly. They are insights that I believe directly apply to you.

1. God expects our immediate and wholehearted response.

I don't know how you would respond if God told you to win a million souls in thirty-six months or ten million souls in a decade. Those numbers were, and still are, astronomical to me. I certainly had not been lagging in effort, energy, or preaching commitments at the time God spoke these words to me. Nevertheless, they did not come in the form of chastisement, nor were they suggestions. They were commands. When a person receives a command from God, there is only one correct response: a quick, immediate, strong "yes" followed up by quick, immediate, and intense action.

Our response must be wholehearted.

2. God wants us to have an urgency for souls.

God never let me work in the ministry without a deep sense of urgency for the salvation of souls. It is the saving of souls that is the highest purpose for any ministry. Miracles, signs, and wonders occur for one ultimate reason: to convince people that Jesus is the Savior.

I have always had, and still have today, an urgent belief that it truly *is* later than we think. Time is limited. Today passes quickly. Tomorrow moves us one day closer to the return of Christ Jesus to this earth and the end of opportunity to accept Him as Savior.

3. God shows us areas where we need to trust Him more.

God also never let me work in the healing ministry without indicating to me areas in which I needed to trust Him more. His words "if you believe, you can conceive" became hallmark words to me.

Through the years I gained a growing understanding of two wonderful passages of the Bible—one in the gospel of Mark, the other in the last book of the Old Testament.

In the gospel of Mark, we are told of an incident in which Jesus encountered a man whose son was influenced by an evil spirit. The demon in this boy kept him from being able to speak, and from time to time, the demon caused him to foam at the mouth, gnash his teeth, and hurl his body into fire, or water, or violently to the ground. Everything had been tried to help this young man and nothing had worked. Jesus said to the father, "If thou canst believe, all things are possible to him that believeth." The father immediately cried out with tears, "Lord, I believe; help thou mine unbelief." Jesus rebuked the foul spirit in the boy and it left him. The boy was freed in an instant. (SEE MARK 9:17–26.)

As I studied this passage I had absolutely no doubt that God's words were for all people throughout all ages: *ALL* things become possible to those who believe. The opposite is also true: virtually nothing gets done if a person refuses or fails to believe.

In the Old Testament, God spoke through the prophet Malachi to His people. He said, "Bring ye all the tithes into the storehouse, that there may be meat in mine house, and prove me now herewith, saith the LORD of hosts, if I will not open you the windows of heaven, and pour you out a blessing, that there shall not be room enough to receive it. And I will rebuke the devourer for your sakes, and he shall not destroy the fruits of your ground; neither shall your vine cast her fruit before the time in the field, saith the LORD of hosts" (MALACHI 3:10–11).

Bringing the tithes into the temple was more than a financial obligation that was part of Jewish religious law. It was a sign of obedience. God had commanded that the tithes be brought. They were part of God's plan for increasing the people and a failure to bring the tithes had resulted in decrease—not only materially, but spiritually.

God reminded the people through His prophet that their obedience in trusting Him—in BELIEVING in Him to the point they were willing to actively serve Him—would cause the "windows" of heaven to be opened to them. What was God going to pour out? Certainly He wasn't going to rain money from heaven. Rather, God rains ideas from heaven. He gives ideas that produce increase, bring blessing, start new trends, create new products, innovate new methodologies, and establish new standards.

Believing releases God's ideas into a person's mind. And at the same time, it shuts down any temptations or detouring thoughts from the person's mind. Belief focuses a person to receive from God all that is necessary for the conception and birth of those "new things"—a new life, a new goal, a new project, a new tactic—that lead to our accomplishing God's plans and purposes for our lives.

I could write an entire book on just these two passages from the Bible but let it suffice at this point for me to conclude: What *you* believe, you can conceive. Believing is the key to having God's next idea for implementation.

I needed to hear that from God in the 1950s, and indeed, He gave me opportunities for dozens of new ideas to be implemented. Some of the ideas produced new ways of answering our mail, new messages to preach to the people, and new ways of conducting our healing crusades. During that decade and in later decades, some of the ideas that God poured into my mind took the form of powerful slogans and expressions that simplified great truths and caused countless millions of people to trust God as they never had before:

- Turn Your Faith Loose

- Get a Point of Contact

- Sow a Seed of Faith

- Make God Your Source of Total Supply

- Something Good Is Going to Happen to You

- Expect a Miracle!

For decades I had a little plaque on my desk that read, MAKE NO LITTLE PLANS HERE. I knew that it would be an act of disobedience for me to pursue anything that fell short of God's best. I am still expecting God to open the windows of heaven and pour new ideas into my mind and heart!

What God said to me is also for you: "If you can BELIEVE, you can CONCEIVE a plan."

4. God wants us to have MORE of Him at all times.

God is the Source of our joy. God is the Source of our pleasure—what delights Him becomes what delights us. God is the Source of our faith.

You might talk yourself into being happy—for a few minutes or hours. You might put yourself into environments that make you happy for a time. But true joy is resident in God and is imparted to us from God. True joy takes root deep in the heart of the person who is in relationship with God. Nothing God calls you to do is intended to become a drudgery or an oppressive burden to you. It is intended for your joy.

There have been times when the healing ministry has been extremely difficult. That is true not only for me, but for every person I've ever known who has placed a high priority on praying for the sick. It is discouraging when not everybody is helped or healed in the way you desire. It is discouraging when people criticize you for praying and expecting God to work healing miracles—claiming

that it is not God's will for people to be healed or that you are an unworthy vessel for God to use. It is discouraging when people second-guess your motives or question your methods. Early in my ministry, some men hid under the platform at one of my crusades, looking for electrical wires that might be sending a "charge" through my body into the people for whom I was praying. A number of deaf children had been healed in that crusade and these skeptics simply could not accept the fact that something wasn't being done to humanly manipulate or cause those healings. How ridiculous! If an electrical charge could cause deaf ears to open, surely such a charge once discovered could and should be put to use in every clinic across America!

There are countless other stories I could tell you—such as the day we lost our tent in a great windstorm in Amarillo or the time when we were forced to leave Australia because of the threat of violence to my ministry team and equipment. Let it suffice to say, I've had the forces of discouragement come against me relentlessly for *decades*. I know that I need the joy of God at work in me, and I need it more and more. The truth is, so do you.

I also need to know more and more that what I am doing is pleasing to God. I need to know at all times that I am in the very center of His will. Now, it is true that if you walk down the center white line of a highway, you are likely to get hit from both sides. That is a good metaphor for what also happens when you walk the center line of God's will. The people of the world who hate God and therefore hate you for following God, will hit you from one side. The people of the church who claim to love God but are jealous of any success you may have, will hit you from the other side. Even so, the walk down the center white line of God's plan and purpose is worth it all if you know that God delights in you and is pleased at what you are doing.

There have been many times when I have had to stop and ask, "God, is this really what You want?" When I know with certainty that it is, I feel His pleasure.

I also have needed to be reminded at various times in my life that God is the Source of my faith. The Bible tells us that we each have been given a measure of faith. The Bible also tells us something that is even more important about our faith: It is our faith directed toward Him that matters, not our faith directed toward a particular problem or a particular goal.

There's a huge and important difference in faith directed *TO* God, and faith aimed toward anyone or anything other than God.

You don't have to believe that a particular thing will happen, or believe that it will happen in a particular way. You just need to believe in God and in His wisdom to know what should happen, how it should happen, and when it should happen.

You don't have to believe that some things will change or that some things will become established. You just need to believe in God and trust Him to change whatever needs to be changed.

You don't have to believe that certain people will do what you want them to do. You just need to believe in God and trust Him to turn the hearts of anybody whose heart needs to be turned.

God is the Source of our faith, and my faith must always be directed to Him as the Source of my total supply. Faith comes from God, and goes back to God.

5. God wants you to INCREASE in every area of your life.

The truth, as difficult as it may seem to us at times, is that God is never through with you, He never allows you to "retire," and He never allows you to rest on your laurels or be satisfied with your own self-prescribed status quo.

God expects growth. He expects us to keep learning and developing all of our lives. He expects us to become more like Christ today than we were yesterday.

It was important for me to hear that God expected me to expand my ministry overseas. I was already conducting periodic crusades

in foreign nations at the time I heard from God. He simply said to me, "Increase."

It was important for me to hear God call me to increase my emphasis on healing. I was already preaching healing. He said to me, "More!"

It was important for me to hear God call me to seek more Partners for Deliverance. I already had generous Partners in large numbers. He said, "Increase."

In these statements, God was telling me to expand my borders, focus my message, and add to the ministry even greater resources of prayer and support. I believe He says those same things to every person. We must always be looking for the ways in which God wants us to reach more people with a more potent message. God's concepts about increase apply to every person, and to every career, business, or ministry endeavor. They are lasting and sure.

Evaluate Your Own Heart

Do you feel an urgency that you are to influence more people to turn to Christ Jesus?

Do you feel an urgency that God is calling you to expand your thinking, expand your efforts, or enlarge your sphere of influence?

Are you willing to move into areas and take on goals that may seem impossible in the natural, trusting God to help you fulfill anything He calls you to do?

Listen.

And listen again.

Listen today.

CHAPTER TEN

The Fullness of God's Call

Success without a successor is failure.

Looking unto Jesus the author and
finisher of our faith.
—HEBREWS 12:2

n the late 1950s, I began to feel a restlessness in me that was very similar to the one I felt before I began the healing ministry. No matter how large the crowds grew, or how many thousands were saved or healed, I felt a certain emptiness that would not go away. I knew God was working to get me out of my comfort zone. I knew that the time was approaching when I had to start building God a university.

I could no longer escape the words God had spoken to me in the back of my brother Elmer's borrowed car on the way to the service where I was miraculously healed from tuberculosis. In an earlier chapter I shared with you God's words to me at that time... but I didn't relate to you the *complete* message. God's complete message was this:

> "Son, I am going to heal you and you are to take My healing power to your generation. You are to build Me a university and build it on My authority and the Holy Spirit."

The last part of God's plan for my life lay dormant in me for more than thirty years, just as the first part of God's plan had been dormant for twelve years. I had *heard* what God said, but frankly, I didn't feel an urgency about building God a university when I was a young man of seventeen, or during my twenties. In many ways, I felt that God's call to build Him a university went far beyond anything in my experience. I also had a sense that building a university would involve a total ministry of God's delivering power, and that my pursuing the first part of God's call on my life—to take God's healing power to my generation—would in some way be the foundation for taking on the second part of God's call.

From the beginning of God's speaking to me, I had a clear understanding that healing resulted in *wholeness*. I also understood that as I established a powerful beachhead for healing—bringing it into the consciousness of people throughout the world—my personal effort would be only a beginning, not an end in itself.

Even though I did not talk about this second part of God's call to me, I never lost sight of it, even when my healing crusades took me across America and to many other nations, and eventually to a major television outreach. The command to build a university was in the inner recesses of my soul. As I traveled, I often took time to visit and study colleges and universities in the cities where we held healing crusades. I visited Stanford, Harvard, Duke, the University of Oklahoma, Oklahoma State University, Wheaton College, UCLA, the University of Southern California, the University of Texas, Emory University, Johns Hopkins University, Vanderbilt University, University of the Pacific, the University of Tennessee, and several universities in foreign nations. On most occasions, I did not merely drive through the campuses, but I spent time whenever possible with the leaders of these great institutions, as well as with professors and students.

In addition, I wrote for information from many more universities. During what I considered to be my leisure hours, I spent time with my wife and children—by this time we had four children, Rebecca, Ronnie, Richard, and Roberta—and I played golf, rode my horse, and poured over the college and university materials sent to me. I talked to architects who had built colleges and universities. I studied how various colleges and universities had come into being, and what had happened to them through the years.

During the late 1950s, I drove with my wife and four children to a farm at the corner of 81st Street and South Lewis Avenue in south Tulsa. I had a strong impression from the Lord that this was the property on which I was to build a university. My family and I would get out of our car, join hands in prayer, and agree in our spirits that God would hold this property until the time came to build.

Occasionally as I preached I referred to building a university based upon God's authority and the Holy Spirit, especially in sermons about Elijah passing his mantle to the young prophet Elisha, and

the priesthood of Eli passing to the young man Samuel. I knew that success without a successor was failure. I could see clearly that a university steeped in the healing ministry and dedicated to an ongoing healing ministry, was God's plan for succession.

Then, in 1961, God spoke directly and strongly in my spirit:

> "Now My time has come for you to build Me a university on My authority and on the Holy Spirit."

I could no longer delay. The time for research and prayer was over. The time for action had come.

The Day We Bought the Land

My spirit jumped within me that the time was near to build. I had no money, no land, no buildings, no faculty, no students, no curriculum, and very little knowledge of how to start. I knew only that I was under the command of Him who has all authority and all power to bring to pass His will. I knew one thing: A university campus needed land.

I called my legal counsel, Saul Yager, to approach the owner of the farm that I believed God had chosen as the site for His university. Saul was a former district judge in Tulsa. In the years he served as our general counsel in the ministry, he became a great friend. At the time I called him, I didn't even know who owned the land. Saul reported back to me that the owner wasn't interested in selling. The land had been in the owner's family for thirty-five years. I insisted that Saul keep trying to buy it until he got it done.

Things dragged on for several weeks. I know that may not seem like a long time to you, but I had an urgency in my spirit and knew God's time had come. Each time Saul approached the owner, he turned him down. Saul finally said, "The man simply won't sell." I knew it was Saul's way of saying, "Give it up." I could not do that.

One day I was in California when the Spirit of the Lord came all over me. That piece of land stood out in my mind as if I were standing there looking at it and walking around on it. In my spirit I could see the groundbreaking, the buildings going up, and the students starting to come. I had a vision into the future when there would be thousands of students going out from the university to take the healing power of Christ to all the world.

I called Saul and said, "Go *today* and buy that land."

Saul said, "Oral, the man won't sell."

I said, "I'm telling you, Saul, I know today is the day. Buy it today."

He said, "If you say so," and we hung up.

Saul called the lawyer who handled the farm owner's legal affairs and he told him about my insistent call. The farm owner's lawyer called the owner and recommended he at least be open to the sale of his land. The owner said, "It is strange you would put it that way. I woke up this morning and decided that if Mr. Roberts' lawyer approached me today, I would sell."

Both Saul and this second lawyer were astonished. To them, this was high drama. Secretly, I believe they knew God was in it and they were inspired to think they were a part of God's plan. Saul later told me, "I think it was a deal done in heaven."

A little while later, the farm owner had second thoughts, but both attorneys reminded him that he had given his word on the deal and he said, "I think you're right," and signed the papers for the sale. There was only one unexpected change the owner wanted in the agreement. He said, "I want a small down payment. I'm also willing for a clause to be included where they can pay it all off at once without penalty."

That suited me just fine! I had only a little down payment to make! As it turned out, we did have sufficient money to pay off the purchase price all at once in the near future. Nobody but God could have foreseen how the financial matters needed to be arranged.

Walking the
Land in Prayer

I'm not ashamed to tell you that I cried out to God from the depths of my soul during the next weeks and months. I wanted desperately to obey His voice. I simply didn't know how. I began to walk back and forth across the bare acres we had just put into escrow with our down payment. As I walked, I called out to God for the knowledge I needed. While I did not know what to do first or how to proceed, I did have these words of assurance that God spoke into my heart:

"I will show you HOW to build My university."

On one particular day, I cried out in a near-desperation tone of voice, "O God, help me! Show me the way!" From the pit of my belly, my spiritual language from the Holy Spirit rose up in me and rolled out of my mouth. I stopped praying in tongues and shifted immediately to praying in English—and I discerned immediately that the words I was speaking were not words that I had thought myself. I felt such a tremendous release in my spirit that I said, "Lord, let me do that again."

It was one of the most electrifying experiences of my entire life. There I was, walking the acres with the squirrels and rabbits and birds as my audience, praying in my spiritual language and interpreting the words back to myself in English. There was a brilliance to those prophetic words that were coming from my mouth—I knew I was receiving revelational knowledge from the Lord.

In the words God gave me, He revealed to me the broad outline of how to build Him a university. He didn't give me all the details, but that afternoon was a great breakthrough into knowledge of how to proceed.

One thing I've learned over the years is not to jump the first time I feel I've heard something from the Lord. I believe strongly that what a person hears in his spirit from the Lord must be tested by the Word of God, by ongoing confirmation from the Spirit, and by sheer practicality. So, as I continued to seek the Lord over the next few weeks, I was excited to find that the revelation God had given me for the university was confirmed again and again to my heart and mind. Words from the Lord rang in my soul:

> "I want you to build My university out of the same ingredient I used when I formed the world, when I created the earth—nothing."

I recalled the verse in the book of Job that says, "He [God] stretcheth out the north over the empty place, and hangeth the earth upon nothing" (JOB 26:7). I was reminded of another verse from the New Testament: "Through faith we understand that the worlds were framed by the word of God, so that things which are seen were not made of things which do appear" (HEBREWS 11:3).

As I walked the acres of the future campus, I had vision after vision. They were vivid, clear, and extremely encouraging to me. I caught a glimpse of a university that was nothing yet...but I could *see it by faith*. I had a very clear understanding that the university would truly be an outstanding educational institution—but with a calling to "educate the whole man" and to be an extension of God's healing power into all the world. I did *not*, however, have any inkling of an idea as to how difficult it all was going to be.

Building on Faith

In the early 1960s we put together a task force led by Dr. John D. Messick, an outstanding educator who was also a man of great faith. He surrounded himself with a group of Ph.D.s to begin to build the curriculum and help recruit the first faculty. I met with this group early on to express to them a basic quarrel I had with the way most universities were structured. Specifically, I had read

in the literature of one university a line that stated, "A university consists of gaining knowledge, adding to it, and passing it on." I told the task force that I had a great problem in thinking that we might create a university in which the mind was elevated above the spirit. I saw that as the main downfall of Adam and Eve in the Garden of Eden—they had sought mental wisdom over faith obedience. I said, "The result has led all mankind to elevate his mind to the point that he does not put God first in his life. As man has elevated his mind above his spirit, he is out of harmony with his Maker and Savior, and also out of harmony with himself."

The men of the task force listened to me with respect. Finally one of them asked, "Exactly how do you expect to build a university that puts the spirit above the mind and yet have it become an accredited university?"

It was the best question they could have asked me. I said, "First, we start with who is in charge of this university—God or man? To me, it is God. Second, who do we believe has all knowledge from the beginning? I say God. Third, we view the raising up of this new university as a command from God whose authority is above all authority. He has chosen through His Holy Spirit to make His Son, Jesus Christ of Nazareth, the real Head of what we build." And then I added, "This will take faith, not reason. If we try to reason it out, it will fail and leave me in disobedience before God. I will have let Him down at the very point where the spiritual is to dominate the mental. But if we believe that God is in our hearts as the Lord of our lives, that He is active in the affairs of mankind, and that He still speaks to us today as He has always done, we can build a university where academic standards will meet or exceed whatever accreditation demands."

God honored the weeks and months we spent integrating spirit and mind, always elevating spirit above mind. I never claimed to be a curriculum expert, but by the Holy Spirit, I was given an understanding beyond myself that the central core of all we offered at the university was to be wrapped around the fact that all truth is in Jesus Christ. We were to make Him the center of the university. We were to look to Him for guidance in everything that was to be done.

In 1962 we broke ground for the first buildings. In 1963 we chartered the university in the state of Oklahoma.

In seeking a charter for the university, we needed to provide a "name" for the university. I never personally sought to have my name on the university. The day came, however, when I could not say "no." God weighed in with His command:

> "Give the university your name, that it may be forever identified with healing. Your name has become synonymous with healing in the world. And this university is never to depart from healing. Make it a neutral place of training, that people may be filled with the Holy Ghost and be like Jesus, and heal the sick as He did. Make it a neutral place; that is, do not let any denominational group control it, not even your own denomination. Choose men of different denominations, men who have been filled with the Holy Ghost, men whose lives are a part of the ministry. Let them be the legal custodians and guardians of this university. Then the people will see that you did not do it, that it was not you yourself that built it, but that it was the Holy Ghost. You must recede, but the ministry must increase."

Those who were Partners for Deliverance in my ministry—many of whom did not have the privilege of going to college but who believed God wanted this kind of university raised up—gave sacrificially to build Oral Roberts University. They wanted what my healing ministry offered to suffering mankind to be at the heart of the campus. They quickly caught the vision of what

ORU might become to the world at large. As the 1960s unfolded, the Partners wanted this even more as they saw student riots taking place on other college campuses across our nation. What we stood for at ORU was faith...dependency upon the Word of God and on the Holy Spirit...and on living with Jesus as our role model of the only "Whole Person" who has ever lived. The Honor Code that was established by the new university board challenged every student, administrator, and faculty member to adopt these core concepts and seek to live them out. The Honor Code continues to be signed by every student, administrator, and faculty member at ORU.

In 1965 we opened our doors to the first three hundred students. These students through the years have told me that they were drawn to the university by a strong desire to be part of God's *solution* in the world, rather than part of the world's *problems*. They came, I believe and they believe, because the Holy Spirit drew them.

In July of 1966, God spoke to me two powerful messages that were related to both the healing ministry and Oral Roberts University. As you read through these two messages, you will see how interrelated the healing ministry and ORU were to be, and are. The first of these messages is quite lengthy. I spoke these words out of my spirit as the Lord poured His words into my spirit during a meeting of approximately fifty people present in the ORU Regents Board Room:

> "I have given you twenty years of taking My healing power to your generation. Now in the rest of the time that I shall give you, I want you to take it even to the remotest bounds of the earth; and not only you but those who are with you, those I have raised up to support and help you.

> "Behold, I shall enlarge your borders and extend your hand to the millions in a harvest of healing where you will seek the lost and suffering. You will

go where they are, even to the remotest areas where My light is seen dim, My voice is heard small, where My healing power is not known. You must find a way to enter into all nations, and I say all nations, with My work of healing. You must divide your work and time in America with the world; this is to be a mighty spreading and gathering.

"You shall suffer much for My glory. You have not been ready for this, but you are ready now. Work with the young, work with the old, work with everyone I shall send to you. Especially raise up your students to hear My voice and to go to the uttermost parts of the earth. Their work will exceed yours and in this, I am pleased. In their success, your ministry will rise to the heights you have always dreamed of. There is much reward ahead, but there is much, much more to be done before the reward comes.

"You shall not be afraid to obey Me. Be not alarmed; be not afraid. This is your hour to move forward with your helpers to penetrate the hearts of millions with My gospel. Turn neither to the right hand nor to the left. Be reliable. Be courageous, always expecting Me to do miracles among the people.

"Millions are waiting for you. Go to them. Again I say, do not be alarmed. I will brighten your way. The people will understand that I am sending you, that I am speaking, that I am working, that I am sending you as My very own chosen vessel. There is no power on earth that can stop you or even hinder you until I say, 'This work is done, and the harvest is gathered.'"

The second time God spoke, I was in Norfolk, Virginia, for a healing crusade. My dear friend, Pat Robertson, was chairman of

the sponsoring pastors for the crusade. He was eating dinner with my wife Evelyn and me one evening and God spoke to me before our meal was finished. His words were so powerful, so dramatic, so far-reaching, and yet so specific that I immediately grabbed paper and pen and wrote them down:

> "Raise up your students to hear My voice, to go where My light is seen dim, where My voice is heard small and My healing power is not known. To go even to the uttermost bounds of the earth. Their work will exceed yours, and in this I am well-pleased."

Those words were ones I was eager to share with all of our administrators, faculty, staff, and students at Oral Roberts University. These words became the hallmark of our mission at Oral Roberts University. In essence, they became ORU's Mission Statement. Today they are referred to as the Founding Vision.

Several years later, in 1970, the university embarked on a campus-wide goal of framing a Statement of Purpose for ORU. The students who participated stated strongly that they believed healing was the core of ORU's purpose. They had come to ORU because of what the ministry had stood for. The faculty and staff also gave their input. In all, more than ninety committee meetings were held on the subject. Through the years, additional committees have met to reevaluate this statement and today, the Statement of Purpose reads:

> It is the purpose of Oral Roberts University, in its commitment to the historic Christian faith, to assist the student in his quest for knowledge of his relationship to God, man, and the universe. Dedicated to the realization of Truth and the achievement of one's potential life capacity, the University seeks to graduate an integrated person—spiritually alive, intellectually alert, socially adept, professionally competent, and physically disciplined.

To accomplish this purpose, Oral Roberts University seeks to synthesize by means of interdisciplinary cross-pollination the best traditions in liberal arts, professional, and graduate education with a charismatic concern to enable students to go into every man's world with healing for the totality of human need.

In many ways, the Statement of Purpose was and is a visionary statement. ORU did not have graduate education or professional degree programs at the time this statement was first written. We did not open our first professional and graduate programs until 1978. The word "charismatic" was just beginning to be voiced in the church world as an outgrowth of what became known as the Charismatic Renewal. The word "charismatic" refers to being Holy Spirit-inspired. Certainly the word applied then to ORU and it continues to apply today. From the beginning, we had placed strong emphasis on integrating spirit, mind, and body, and on enabling students to go into all the world. Those purposes remain.

I share that statement with you today for this reason: The Statement of Purpose was a statement put together—ably and completely—by a group of Spirit-led individuals working together under God's guidance. It was and is, however, a manmade statement based upon God-inspired words. The Mission Statement of ORU was voiced directly from God to my spirit.

There is no comparison in the power of these statements and their impact on human hearts.

Just a few months ago I had dinner with a graduate of Oral Roberts University and this person, now in his late fifties, quoted to me the Mission Statement of ORU verbatim.

I said, "How do you remember that?"

He said, "How could I forget it? It's what drew me to ORU. The Mission Statement of ORU became the mission statement for my life. And, I know I'm not alone in that. Hundreds of ORU alumni could quote those words to you without any review or prompting. We *know* as graduates of Oral Roberts University that we were raised up to hear God's voice and then to go where God's light is seen dim, His voice is heard small, and His healing power is not known...even to the uttermost bounds of the earth. Everywhere I go around the world—to more than thirty nations now—I see ORU graduates doing what God raised us up as alumni to do. They are everywhere, it seems, with the Gospel of Jesus Christ and the power of the Holy Spirit. They are taking healing wherever they go, in thousands of unique and exciting ways. They are changing churches and cities and nations."

God had told me that the work of the students who came through Oral Roberts University would exceed mine. I have no doubt of it.

My successors are those who have a form of "spiritual DNA" for the healing ministry imparted to them by God Almighty. They are presently around the world taking a message of whole-person healing—spirit, mind, and body— into every avenue of life.

God said He would be "well-pleased" at their work. I am, too.

What God's Words to Me Mean to Your Life Today

There are several things that I want you to note in the words of God to me. But first, I want to say this: There may be something that you have harbored for many years in your life that you *know* is part of God's plan and purpose for you. It is something you know deep within you that you are to accomplish. You may never have voiced it before, or you may have voiced it only to a few close family members or friends. My word to you today is this: NOW may very well be the time for you to begin acting in earnest and with all of your efforts to fulfill that word of the Lord in your heart. God may very well be using this book and your reading of it in this hour to speak to you, "Now is the time."

As you begin to act to fulfill God's *complete* purpose for your life, be encouraged.

1. All that came before has brought you to the point of what now can be.

Do not be discouraged that you may not have done *yet* all that you know God has designed for you to do from even before your birth. All that you have done in the past—including all the experiences you have had, all that you have learned, all of the associations you have developed, all the dreams that have continued to build in your heart and mind, all the places you have gone and the conversations you have had, especially meaningful, heartfelt conversations with godly men and women about the eternal principles of God—have brought you to this moment. Consider how God has prepared you and positioned you.

Nothing is wasted in God's economy. Everything about your past can be used by God as building blocks for your future. Trust Him with your previous mistakes. Give Him your previous successes. And ask Him to use you NOW to do all that He has designed you to do.

2. Do not give in to fear.

I don't know any person who lives totally without fear, especially if God is calling that person to a task that the person knows in his right mind is too great for his personal talents, intellect, or resources.

Fear, however, is the opposite of faith. Fear can paralyze a person into doing nothing.

In order to act with strength in the face of fear you must first be thoroughly convinced that God is telling you what to do and that now is the time. He will confirm His plan and purpose to you. You may feel an inner restlessness, as I did. You may find that the

word of God seems to speak to your situation every time you pick up your Bible or every time you hear a message from a person who truly speaks with the power of God at work in his or her life. God will give you an urgency about what you are to do if you are to act *immediately*. He will also give you an understanding about what you might still need to learn or put into place if you are to act in the near future, but not immediately.

The Bible tells us that Queen Esther was afraid when she realized the enormity and danger connected to a task God was asking her to undertake. Confronting her husband the king, about the trickery of one of the king's closest advisors, could have cost her everything, including her life. Esther sent word to her uncle, asking for his advice. He sent back this message: "Who knoweth whether thou art come to the kingdom for such a time as this?" Esther took courage and replied to his words, asking her uncle and the people of God to fast and pray for her, and then she said, "I will go in unto the king, which is not according to the law: and if I perish, I perish." (SEE ESTHER 4:13–16.)

You must come to the place of sold-out commitment: I will do what God has commanded me to do, and leave all the consequences to God.

In the early 1960s I faced an extremely difficult situation as we prepared for a healing crusade in Miami, Florida. Threats were made against my life and ministry that were very real, and imminent. God spoke to me these words:

> "Do not fear these men. If you were put in jail it would not hurt your ministry. I have given you a strong and solid ministry, and I Myself am with you. I am not through with your crusades yet. You are to continue strongly and press forward in the crusades."

It's one thing to have words of encouragement from other people— especially if they aren't the ones who are going to reap the full consequences of what might happen. It's entirely different when a person hears God say, "Do not fear!" I took courage at what *God* said to me, and I proceeded with our crusade and saw thousands of souls saved and people healed who might not otherwise have come to Christ or experienced healing had I given in to fear. The threat against me never materialized.

I don't know what you may be facing in the form of threats from other people, or fears related to your own inadequacies. I do know this. If God says to you, "Fear not!", He is sending you a signal that He is totally in charge of the situation and He will honor your faithful efforts and defeat any enemy that comes against you.

God never told me that I would be free from all criticism and doubts from people around me. In fact, God clearly told me in the building of ORU—as well as at other times in my life and ministry—that I was going to be in for a rough ride and significant suffering.

In reality, some of the strongest opposition I had when it came to establishing Oral Roberts University came from the top-level leaders on the staff of the Oral Roberts Evangelistic Association! In part, these leaders did not fully grasp the vision of ORU as a means of taking God's healing power to the world. In part, they were struggling with what establishing a university might mean to their jobs. We had several heated but productive meetings about the future direction of the ministry, and eventually these men were not only on board but were enthusiastic as we established ORU.

Certainly, there was criticism, scoffing, and even a certain amount of threatening from people in the greater Oklahoma community who genuinely thought a healing evangelist could never, and therefore should never, establish a fully accredited university.

If I had allowed those who disagreed with me or who misunderstood me to instill fear in me, I would have failed because I never would have taken the first step forward. Don't allow those

who may be skeptical or critical of you to keep you from acting. Fear not!

3. You have the faith necessary for God to build what is important to Him.

You may not have anything *but* faith, but let me assure you, with faith in God, you are connected to the One who has *everything* necessary.

Don't try to reason out what seems to be a "logical plan" according to what others have done. Don't try to predict on the basis of reason or statistics what your outcome may be.

Certainly I am not telling you to set your mind aside. What I am saying to you is this: Ask God to give you His mind! Ask Him to help you think as He thinks! God wants to use you in ways that He may never have used anybody before. God doesn't use statistical analyses, historical precedent, or probability tables to predict your success. God has a way and He will show it to you if you will place all your trust in Him. Remember always this truth from God's Word: "Trust in the LORD with all thine heart; and lean not unto thine own understanding. In all thy ways acknowledge him, and he shall direct thy paths" (PROVERBS 3:5–6).

4. Recognize that God has a plan of succession for anything He calls you to do.

What God does, lasts. Anything new that God establishes on this earth has a seed of eternal benefit in it because it has part of God's own Spirit in it. What you do for the Lord is intended to extend into the future.

You cannot predict fully how God's plan of succession will unfold. That is an area for your faith! But you can be certain that what God establishes—and what He allows to grow, flourish, and multiply—will *never* be destroyed by the enemy of your soul. God rebukes the devourer, not only for the sake of those who plant and cultivate God's harvest fields, but so that the devourer cannot destroy those things that bring glory and honor to Him.

Trust God to raise up your successors, and if you have the privilege of helping those successors during your lifetime, do so to the utmost of your ability.

Evaluate Your Own Heart

Is today the day to begin a lifelong dream and plan that you know is from God?

Do you struggle with doubts that your past might keep you from God's future? Do you struggle with fear rooted in what people might say to you or about you, or what they might do to try to stop you from succeeding at God's plan?

Are you trusting God to supply *all* that you need to fulfill His purposes for your life?

Listen.

And listen again.

Listen today.

CHAPTER ELEVEN

No Limits!

God wants to expand your understanding of Him, and your horizons.

The LORD will perfect that which concerneth me:
thy mercy, O LORD, endureth for ever; forsake not
the works of thine own hands.

—PSALM 138:8

don't know any person who has ever accused me of thinking too small. The exact opposite seems to have been true for much of my life and ministry. Countless people through the years have told me that they thought I was thinking too big, too grand, too extravagant. Maybe I was. But then again, maybe I wasn't. Maybe I just happened to have a glimpse of a God who specializes in doing the impossible!

Lee Braxton—who was the founding chairman of the ORU Board of Regents and a dear friend for many years—told me one time that he had literally cut the word *impossible* out of his dictionary. That stuck with me.

Throughout my ministry, from the earliest days, I knew and believed the words Jesus gave to His followers about the use of their faith: "Nothing shall be impossible unto you" (MATTHEW 17:20). I also knew that I had seen God do amazing things. I had seen Him create a hip socket in a young man who had no hip socket. He had raised back to life a woman who from all appearances was dead, even to the point that her body had stiffened and her limbs could not be moved by outward force. I had seen God work with flawed but willing human beings to establish a university based on His authority. God seemed to be continually revealing new insights to me about His goodness and greatness, and to be taking my healing ministry to new heights.

It came as something of a surprise to me in the late 1960s and early 1970s when God spoke to me repeatedly, telling me that I wasn't thinking "big enough."

In May 1968, God spoke to me twice, and in so doing, He radically changed the way I approached my ministry. He said:

> "I said unto you ALL nations. By My Spirit. Every Christian is to be a missionary Christian. Put on a bigger coat."

Later that same year He said:

> "Go into every man's world."

Up to this point in my ministry, I had been to a number of nations and I had a heart for reaching people in foreign lands. As I wrote in the previous chapter, God had said to me two years before this, "You must find a way to enter into all nations, and I say all nations, with My work of healing." I admit to you that I had not truly paid enough attention to the word ALL. "All" is such a little word that encompasses so much! Especially when a person is contemplating taking the gospel to all the nations of the world.

God showed me in a visual example that when a person puts on a coat that is too small, he feels cramped and restrained—he cannot move freely. When a person puts on a coat that fits perfectly, he feels comfortable—but in that, a person might become too relaxed and too complacent. It is when God leads a person to put on a "bigger" coat that the person comes face to face with the challenge of growing. I knew clearly that God intended for me to grow personally in my understanding of Him, and for the ministry to grow in its outreach. And, most important, I knew that neither my understanding nor our ministry outreach would grow according to human efforts alone. It would be "by His Spirit." More than ever before, I felt compelled to rely upon the Holy Spirit to lead me.

Later in 1968, when God said that we were to go into every person's world, I immediately began to put the pieces together.

Note that this was in the 1960s. There was only one way for a person to speak to all nations in any given lifetime. There was only one way to enter into every person's world, which I interpreted to mean the places where the people were (in the comfort of their homes), not necessarily the places where we ministers wanted people to be (in churches or auditoriums where the gospel was being preached).

The one way to reach all the world, and to reach into every person's world, was television.

A Front-Row Seat
at All the Crusades

I was no stranger to the world of television. My first experiences with television came in the early 1950s. I knew the largest tent we had ever used seated only twelve thousand people—and perhaps several thousand more by means of loudspeaker if overflow crowds stood around the edges of the tent. We could hold fourteen crusades a year—we were limited to that number because it took a significant amount of time to set up, tear down, and transport the massive cathedral tent and all of the chairs and equipment necessary for an outdoor service. We were limited in our crusades to major population centers in order to reach the maximum numbers of people at any given time.

I also knew that there were 26 million television sets in the United States in the early 1950s and the number was growing every day. Television was a new and exciting medium and people were anxious to watch virtually *anything* that might be broadcast.

After several months of preparation, and then working and filming in a studio, our first television program premiered on January 10, 1954. It was carried by sixteen stations. The response was immediate—overnight the number of people writing to me for prayer soared.

As effective as the first programs *appeared* to be in the eyes of some, I found something profoundly lacking in them. There was a "wooden" quality about them that was stifling. I felt ineffective.

During this time, Rex Humbard of Akron, Ohio, encouraged me to find a way to film directly in the big tent. That was what I wanted, too, but I didn't know how to get the job done. I arranged for NBC to send a team from New York to one of our crusades and make recommendations. They came back with a very simple professional assessment: "It can't be done." Well, I had heard that line before when it came to the use of technology, and I refused to accept it.

We continued to search and we finally found a film company that agreed to try taping a crusade service on location. Their bid for the job was $42,000. We certainly didn't have that kind of money, but I asked them to come anyway to our next crusade and they said they would. Then came the hard part—where to get the money. I began to study the Bible and after much prayer, I felt that I had an idea from God. We called it the "Blessing Pact."

I called a meeting and invited those who had expressed an interest in seeing us go on television. I shared with the people several instances in the Bible in which people had been blessed by God in the aftermath of their giving. I then said to this group, "I am asking four hundred and twenty people in this audience to pledge a hundred dollars each. I want you to let me enter into a Blessing Pact with you for one year. I will use your gift to win souls."

I explained to them what I believed about giving—that I regarded it as a seed that a person planted. I encouraged them to expect God to meet their needs as they planted a seed to win souls. And I said, "I will earnestly pray that the Lord will return your gift in its entirety from a totally unexpected source." I also said these words, shocking my associates as much as I shocked those in the audience: "I promise at the end of one year if God has not blessed you, I will return your money." I had absolutely no doubt that God would bless those who trusted Him for a blessing. The people responded enthusiastically to accept my challenge and enter into that first Blessing Pact. The response was sufficient for us to get started.

(By the way, two people later wrote for their money back. I sent it. One of them sent my reimbursement check right back and wrote, "I only wanted to see if you would keep your word.")

I had initial concerns about how the people who attended the crusades would respond to big, bright, hot lights positioned throughout the tent, and to the cameras, recording devices, cables, and crewmen who would be doing the filming. I knew some people might feel it sacrilegious to bring cameras into a worship service.

Even though I was extremely eager to get the filming done right, I was even more concerned that the people might be disturbed to the point that they would be less responsive to the invitation to be saved or to the releasing of their faith for healing.

My fears were groundless. There was a freedom in the service I could not explain, and the responses to both the salvation invitation and healing line were tremendous. Dramatic healings were filmed for the first time in history, one right after another.

The first program in this new format aired in February 1955. Television stations were totally unprepared for the response they received. Their switchboards were jammed, their mail unprecedented. It shook up some station managers so much, they canceled our program—and then they really began to get mail! Millions of people expressed excitement about our program and wanted it shown on their favorite station.

One particular healing that came out of that early television programming seemed to make the front page of every major newspaper, including the papers in Los Angeles, Chicago, Dallas, and New York. Anna Williams was a young woman who had been involved in a train-car wreck. Shortly after she was released from the hospital—after surgery and complications with blood clots—she was stricken with polio. She went back into the hospital and endured many days of pain and therapy—this time, also fighting for the safe delivery of her unborn child. Then, after she was released from the hospital the second time, she gave birth but was crippled anew by spondylitis, a disease similar to polio. This left her confined to a wheelchair.

Anna watched the program of one of our crusade services from her wheelchair in her living room. When I asked those in the television audience to place one hand on their heart and pray for their healing even as I prayed for them, Anna did so. In that precise moment, the Holy Spirit entered her body and she had an overpowering compulsion to get up and walk. She asked for her husband's help and he walked over and took her hand. To his surprise, she pulled herself up and began to take tentative steps. These steps became bolder and stronger and very quickly, she was walking the length of the room, praising God the entire time. She lifted her toddler son and raised him high over her head for the first time in the boy's twenty-eight months of life. Then she got down on the floor and played with him for the first time. When she sprang to her feet again, her joy at being able to move so freely caused her to dance around the room!

Very quickly, everybody in Wichita Falls knew about the miracle that had happened on Eighth Street as Anna Williams watched Oral Roberts on television and prayed with him when he prayed.

Her testimony made people even hungrier to see the miracles of God and to hear about a God who desires to give miracles to all who will believe.

I personally was surprised at how many people watched our programs on television in the 1950s. I knew that television was the way to get the message of God's delivering power to more people—I just hadn't realized how effective television was going to be.

I was also surprised at *who* watched our programs. Years later when I met President John F. Kennedy in the White House, he said to me, "Reverend Roberts, I have seen you on television and I enjoy it very much." He was only one of many well-known personalities who spoke similar words to me down through the years.

A New Format for a New Generation

By 1962, I was once again feeling dissatisfied with the television programs. They continued to be well-received and interest in them continued to grow, but I became disenchanted with their quality. Television had developed rapidly and was becoming amazingly sophisticated. Viewers began to expect higher and higher

production standards in the programs they watched. I didn't feel that we had kept pace with the industry. I also didn't like what I thought was an overemphasis on my hands. It seemed to me that the reading of Holy Scripture, my sermons, and the prayers for the unsaved were presented as incidental to my hands being laid on the sick. Plus, many of my sermons were being filmed in studios, although the healing lines were filmed at the crusades. I had become accustomed to television so that a studio setting no longer affected my preaching. But the format for the programs overall really hadn't advanced. I met with our producers and directors, but things changed very little.

At that same time, ORU was in its birth stages, and I did not feel the time was right to get involved in a totally new television ministry. We began to cut back on areas of the nation where our programs had weak reception and response. Finally, in 1965, I made the decision to be completely off television by the summer of 1967. One-half of the stations were dropped in 1966 and the remainder in May of 1967.

It was one of the toughest decisions of my ministry. My staff was horrified—and began citing statistics and growth. I was unimpressed. I refused to be married to any method and I knew the time for this particular one had passed. I also knew that we needed to be off television for a sufficient length of time so that interest might become heightened for any new format God might lead us to develop, in the event that we decided to return to television someday.

And then God spoke. I knew we needed to get back on the air as quickly as possible, but in a brand-new way.

Not long after God spoke, I had lunch out on the West Coast with Ralph Carmichael. Ralph was one of the outstanding conductors and arrangers in the music business at that time and his arrangements for stars such as Nat King Cole, Roger Williams, and others won him critical acclaim from musicians and fans alike. Best of all,

Ralph was a committed Christian. He had arranged the music for our radio programs for some time.

Ralph brought a friend of his, Dick Ross, to our lunch. Dick was founder and president of Worldwide Pictures and had produced and directed the majority of the motion pictures and television programs of the Billy Graham Evangelistic Association. By the time of our lunch meeting, he had been working for some time in the secular television industry, producing and directing popular shows and prime-time specials. Dick was eager to do a totally new kind of religious television show. When he began to tell me about what he envisioned, I knew I had found the right man.

The more we talked—not only that day but in the coming weeks—and the more I prayed and listened for God's confirming words, the more the pieces began to fit together. I had a confidence that our programs in a new format would reach the church world. I also had an excitement that our programs might be able to reach into *every person's world*. To do that, we would need the best-known stars in the business, prime-time program slots, top-flight production, and exciting music.

The year before this, we had put together a team of outstanding young singers at Oral Roberts University. They took the name World Action Singers. They traveled with me in sixteen different nations overseas and they were a smash hit with the old and young everywhere we went. They had a NOW sound. My son Richard worked with them and, together with Ralph Carmichael, the World Action Singers not only were groomed for television, but also adopted a limited amount of choreography (especially by today's standards). That shocked some, but the choreography also did a great deal to attract the unchurched audience we were hoping to reach.

A programming format finally emerged. We decided to tape weekly programs at ORU for viewing on Sunday mornings. Our major thrust, however, would be quarterly prime-time specials that would

be taped at the NBC studios in Burbank, California. The specials would feature famous guests, spectacular sets and wardrobes, new music—the "works"! We named the specials "CONTACT!"

We taped a pilot program featuring Mahalia Jackson as our guest star. Mahalia had been a warm friend of mine for years and I felt extremely fortunate that she was willing to participate and was not booked at the time of our taping. Then, the media reps began trying to place the show. Most station managers were dubious, but once they saw our pilot tape, they changed their minds.

Our first special aired in March 1969 and was shown in every state and all the provinces of Canada. It created a sensation in the religious field, but more importantly for me, I knew we had found a way of getting the attention of the unchurched. The first half of the program was attention-getting. The music and sets kept the audience with us for the second half of the show, during which I gave a message and prayed for the needs of the people.

The mail response to the program was profound. People who had never written before wrote to ask for prayer and give their support for this new type of program. We had landed in the middle of a powerful flowing stream.

Our subsequent prime-time specials featured such outstanding performers as Pat Boone, Anita Bryant, Dale Evans, Jerry Lewis, Jimmy Durante, Lou Rawls, Kay Starr, Sarah Vaughn, and Jimmy Rogers—some of the biggest names in entertainment in that era. We taped a Christmas show and produced specials for Easter, Thanksgiving, Valentine's Day, and a program especially for youth. Some of our programs featured footage from locations that were far from Tulsa, Oklahoma— Alaska and Japan among them.

We reached as many as 50 million viewers with one of our specials—an amazing number at the time. Many people who saw us first on our prime-time specials began to watch our Sunday-morning programs. And, many young people who had never before considered attending Oral Roberts University, began to write for information.

Although it didn't happen right away, our television programs began to be aired in other nations. Today, I have absolutely no doubt that we have been seen or heard—by means of radio, television, or Internet broadcast—in every nation.

All Kinds of Miracles

There was a dimension to going into "every person's world" that I began to see more clearly a few years after we went back on television with a new format. In 1972, while flying to a television-taping session out in California, God spoke these words:

> "Turn loose! Turn loose! Pray for all kinds of miracles!"

I knew instantly that going into every person's world also meant touching every person's need. Up to that point in my ministry, I had openly acknowledged, addressed, and preached messages of healing and deliverance for spiritual and physical needs. When God spoke to me about "all kinds of miracles," I automatically had to ask myself, "Does God have miracles for other areas of life?" The answer, of course, is a resounding "YES!"

I began to preach that God has miracles for our financial and material needs. Although some in the church world have proclaimed that God has a special love for the poor, I searched the Scriptures diligently and found no proof of that. God's desire from the beginning has been to bless the people who put their trust in Him by giving them not only sufficiency for their needs, but an overflow so that they might be a blessing to others around them. Although some in the church world have proclaimed that Jesus was impoverished, I searched the Gospels diligently and found no proof of that. Jesus had all of His needs met everywhere He went. While He did not have a permanent home of His own—in truth, this *world* was never His home—Jesus always had a place to sleep,

food to eat, a garment to wear that was seamless and in the ancient world, very valuable, and sufficient resources to travel with a small band of men and women who were His close ministry associates.

I began to preach that God has miracles for our families and for our churches. He has miracles for our minds and emotions. He has creative miracles and restorative miracles. I saw that the main challenge that lies before us is to turn our faith loose to believe God for *every* miracle He is sending our way. His miracles are unlimited in number, type, and scope.

I began to preach that miracles are for every day.

I preached that miracles are coming toward us or passing by us—it is our privilege to reach out and receive what God has for us.

I preached that a miracle settles the issue—miracles solve problems in our lives so we might help others around us solve problems in their lives.

I preached that what we give becomes a seed of our faith that God multiplies into a harvest of miracles—giving back to us exactly what we need most. Therefore, when we give, we can turn our faith loose to God to trust Him for *precisely* the miracle we need.

The bottom line is that we must never limit what God wants to do for us, in us, around us, or through us. We must be open to all ways in which He might be seeking to expand our horizons, enlarge our faith, multiply our harvest, and increase our influence on this earth.

We are limited only because *we* put limits on a limitless God.

What God's Words to Me Mean to Your Life Today

I believe from the depths of my being that God has *more* for you. He not only has more for you to do, but He wants to enlarge in you your understanding of Him and His limitless power and provision. What God spoke to me has at least three applications to your life.

1. God has more people for you to reach with the good news

God has more people for you to reach with a message that God loves, God heals, God is the Source of every person's total supply, and God sent His only begotten Son so that any person who believes in Him might be forgiven of sin and live with God for all eternity.

God may not call you to television or to a public ministry of any kind. But regardless of the nature and scope of His plan for you and the methods He calls you to pursue in fulfilling that plan, God has *more* people for you to reach with the gospel than you are presently reaching. He desires that you touch more people with His healing power that makes a human being whole.

Look around you.

See the opportunities.

Explore the potential that lies just beyond your current grasp.

To whom might God be sending you?

In what ways might He be speaking to your heart to give more of yourself away to others in need?

Where might He desire for you to go, and for what purpose?

In what ways is God calling you to turn yourself inside-out for the sake of Christ Jesus?

So many people in our world today are turning inward. Perhaps in fear of unseen assault, fear of unpredictable financial markets, fear of failure, fear of insufficient funds, or fear of rejection, people everywhere seem to be hoarding their resources—not only their money but their talents, their love, and their compassion. They are living inside themselves rather than reaching out. True, many are involved in volunteer activities in temporary, short-term ways. I'm not talking about an occasional benevolent activity. I'm talking about having a perspective of being continually willing to give something of yourself to help any person with need who crosses your path.

It may mean reaching out to your neighbor next door.

It may mean helping a television evangelist go on a missionary trip overseas.

It may mean visiting people in the hospital.

It may mean offering to pray for a person in your church whom you see crying on bended knee at the altar rail.

It may mean giving your talent to encourage those who desire to learn but can't afford lessons.

There are millions of ways of giving, as many ways as there are people and opportunities.

The Bible makes no mention of an acceptable retirement age. It gives no acceptable excuses for a failure to pray, tell others about Jesus, or give what has been placed into our hands as a resource.

Listen for the ways God will tell *you* to extend the gospel.

2. The time may have come for you to shift to a new method.

There's an old phrase, "The bloom is off the rose." I believe that is a truth that applies to every method at some point. Methods come and go. They may work very effectively for a period of time, but then they become less effective. The challenge facing all of us is to stay ahead of that curve and to know when to let go of an old method and embrace a new one.

Only God knows the most effective method for you to use in fulfilling your purpose on this earth *now*, and *in the future*. Only God can look down the road and see what will "work best" for you in the coming months and years.

Expect God to give you a glimpse into the future so that you might adjust your methods. Ask Him to show you how best to prepare for the changes that are coming your way.

3. Begin to expect miracles every day, in every area of your life...as you have never expected before.

A miracle happens when God sovereignly intervenes in the normal course of human life—either by altering the natural and physical world, including the laws of time, or by altering a human heart. God sends miracles of healing, miracles of provision and protection, creative ideas, financial windfalls, renewed ability to love, changes in perspective and attitude, and new friendships. In countless ways, God desires to cause miraculous changes for *good* in every area of your life.

Never assume that you can do anything solely on your own strength of intellect, physical prowess, or ingenuity.

Never assume that you can or should do anything solely by yourself.

Never assume that you know better than God how to resolve any difficulty or problem you face.

God has built into every one of us a need for Him, and as we turn our faith loose to trust Him, He enlarges us, continually giving us an added capacity to receive and give from His infinite resources.

God has just the miracle you need to get through today, and to prepare for tomorrow.

Evaluate Your Own Heart

Is it time for a change of methodology—in your personal life, in your business or ministry, in your church outreach programs?

Is today the day you need to reach out to others in a new way?

Is there someone God is leading you to engage in a conversation with, or to pray for, or to help in some practical way?

Listen.

And listen again.

Listen today.

CHAPTER TWELVE

Merging Methods in Faith

Some methods can be combined for greater effectiveness. All methods are activated fully by faith.

[Jesus said,] They that are whole need not a
physician, but they that are sick.
—MATTHEW 9:12

In 1974 during a healing service, God reminded me of the message of Jesus, "They that are sick need a physician," but then He shocked me by speaking these words to my spirit:

> "I want you to raise up Christian doctors who will accept My healing power in its fullness. They will do all they can through prayer and they will do all they can through medicine. They will both treat the sick and pray for the people and they will be accepted as your representatives to take My healing power to your generation. Yes, I will use them to touch thousands who otherwise will live in darkness of superstition, witch doctors, spiritism, and demon worship. Not only will they be extensions of My Son Jesus but they will be extensions of My call to you to take My healing power to your generation."

All my life I have had a great appreciation for physicians and others in the medical world. I have had a number of major surgeries in my life, and have been under the regular care of physicians for routine exams. Unlike many people in the religious denomination in which I grew up, I have always believed strongly in the role that physicians have in God's healing processes. From my perspective, *all* healing comes from God. He uses many methods, and many "instruments"— including skilled specialists—to heal. Prayer is one method. Medicine is one method. Faith applies to *all* methods.

As has been true for nearly all instances in which God challenged me to undertake something new, and outside my level of expertise, I waited for God's confirmation and I waited until God said, "Now."

By 1975, Oral Roberts University was fully accredited and growing at a rapid rate of success. I felt strongly led to add graduate schools to the mission of ORU.

All my life I have believed there are four inescapable professions that every person must deal with in life: theology, law, medicine, and business. Education is central to each of these professions. These professions are like four corners that come together to impact a person's life. They obviously are areas in which a Christian can be effective in taking God's healing power into "every person's world."

In approaching the challenge of adding health-care graduate education to ORU, I gathered top medical people around me—men and women I knew were Spirit-filled, and who were willing to risk their medical reputations to establish a Christ-centered, Holy Spirit-based medical school. I knew from the start the task of adding medical training to the educational program at ORU was not going to be easy. As anticipated, we got hit from both sides.

To many in the medical world I was still a "healing evangelist" and it really didn't matter how much I personally had studied or what I had accomplished; they saw my healing ministry as a stumbling block. On the other side, there were a great many Pentecostal and charismatic leaders who saw my inclusion of medicine as a denial of sorts of direct supernatural healing from God in response to faith and prayer.

A well-known and influential physician, an orthopedic surgeon, crossed my path at precisely the right time. Dr. James Winslow and his wife Sue had both overcome serious illness and injury through a combination of prayer and medicine. Jim and I had numerous conversations about prayer, about the medical community and medical education, and especially about the full meaning of these two scriptures:

- "But my God shall supply all your need according to his riches in glory by Christ Jesus" (PHILIPPIANS 4:19).
- "I am the Lord that healeth thee" (EXODUS 15:26).

Jim shared with me his experiences in the operating room and in his dealing with severely injured patients. I shared with Jim my

experiences in praying for the sick. We agreed on this central point: It is God who heals. Stated another way: All healing comes from God.

People have asked, "But what about supernatural intervention?" I believe it comes in two main ways. One, God acts entirely on His own without anybody doing anything. That doesn't happen often. Two, a believer or a group of believers prays with faith, and agrees in prayer, for God to heal a sick person or destroy a disease. That is the way supernatural healing most often happens as I know it.

I am also familiar with receiving healing through the principles and processes of medicine. Although it was rarely recognized at that time, faith is no less a factor! Every time I have been under medical care by a doctor, or in a hospital as a patient, I have gone into that situation with my faith in *God*—basing my hope for a cure on God as my Source working through the physician, the nurses, the medicine, and medical equipment. Never once have I looked to any man, however skilled, or to any medical facility, whatever the state of the art or the reputation of the facility, as the Source of my recovery or health. God is my Source of healing at all times and in all situations.

I came to the strong conclusion decades ago that when a person is sick, he must avail himself of *both prayer and medicine,* and to seek out the best of both of these methods, trusting at all times that God is the Healer.

In 1975, we announced our plan to open a School of Theology, a School of Business, a School of Law, and a School of Medicine at ORU—and to open these schools in 1978. The School of Medicine was to be flanked by a School of Dentistry and a School of Nursing. Everybody seemed to applaud the existence of the first three professional graduate schools listed above. They didn't have much of a problem with nursing, or even with dentistry. But when it came to medicine, we were in for the fight of our lives. I had a driving force to obey God. There were some in the medical world who felt a sudden driving force to stop me.

It wasn't enough that we were attracting an outstanding medical faculty and building some of the finest science facilities in the nation. In order for a school of medicine to be successful, it had to have affiliation agreements with one or more hospitals so the students might gain practical clinical experience. Therein lay the problem. None of the local hospitals were willing to take our students, given our mandate to combine prayer and medicine.

Now, I want to be very clear on one point. A number of physicians at that time were praying *for* their patients—usually back in the quiet solitude of their offices as they looked at a patient's chart. Very few physicians, apart from those who worked at Loma Linda University in southern California, seemed willing to pray openly *with* their patients. Some claimed that they didn't want to violate their patients' religious beliefs, some were too embarrassed or bashful, and others seemed to believe that prayer from a physician implied a lack of confidence in medical science. Whatever the reason, physicians were not routinely praying with patients. Hospital chaplains prayed with patients, and occasionally nurses seemed to be praying with patients (usually when nobody was overhearing them). And perhaps more importantly, very few physicians regarded prayer as being an effective method of healing *on par with medicine*. Those physicians who did pray saw prayer as supplemental to medical care, not equal to it as a delivery system of God's healing power.

The hospitals in the area surrounding ORU knew that we were serious about elevating prayer so that it stood on equal footing with medicine in the care of those who were ill. They wanted nothing to do with that approach.

Jim said to me, "The option is to find hospitals outside Tulsa. There may be a few. It may be difficult to extend the School of Medicine clinical training to other cities, but it may be doable." And then Jim added these words: "If we are to open the School of Medicine by 1978, God is going to have to step in and do something supernatural."

It happened in a way I had never anticipated.

Rain Upon Our Desert

In February 1977, our precious elder daughter Rebecca and her husband Marshall were killed in a tragic air crash. Our grief was devastating—sudden and overwhelming. Only a parent who has lost a child can begin to fathom the depth of our pain and sorrow. I also felt the devil mocking me: "You have said God is a good God. Where is He now?" I didn't know fully how to answer that question in my intense grief, but I also knew that the first words out of my mouth when I was given the news of the plane crash had been, "God knows something about this that we don't know." My friend, that is the truth in all cases of loss that we cannot explain. God is with us, even when we do not comprehend Him or understand His purposes.

After my wife Evelyn and I had arranged for the care of the three children Rebecca and Marshall left behind, and after the memorial service in their honor, we decided that we would go to the California desert for a time of quiet personal grieving and reflection. Through the years I had gone to the desert on several occasions when I was facing special needs. In the vast quietness of the desert, I had been able to reach out to God and reflect on what He had called me to do.

Our first evening in the desert, the voice of God came roaring in my head:

"I will rain upon your desert!"

I quickly asked Evelyn to give me paper to write on. She handed me a little notebook with several blank pages and as rapidly as God's words came to my spirit, I began writing them down. I knew that God had something powerful and monumental to say to me.

I had a strong visual image to go with these first words of God to me. On a prior trip to the desert, I had witnessed what seemed to me to be a tremendous miracle of God's life-giving power. The land had seemed stark and barren to me as we arrived in the desert on that prior trip—the shifting sands, the gullies, the scars on the environment. I saw trackless miles beneath the burning sun and felt that the land was crying for rain…crying…yes, crying. Then, a great cloudburst had poured down on the parched land and almost overnight we saw life bursting like an explosion from the cracked and dusty ground. Long-dried-up vegetation seemed to leap into newness of greenery. Tiny flowers burst from nowhere. I recalled the Bible verse that says, "The desert shall rejoice, and blossom as the rose" (ISAIAH 35:1).

God continued to speak:

> "Now is the time! Son, you cannot put the vision I have given you into a place where My full healing power is not freely accepted. It must not be in a place defeated by a lack of faith in My miraculous power.… The healing streams of prayer and medicine must merge through what I will have you build. Every physician, every nurse, every person praying, must be in harmony with My calling to you in the healing ministry. All medical and surgical skill, all research for a cure for cancer and other diseases destroying man must be carried on in an atmosphere of prayer and a total dependence upon Me as the Source of healing and life. You build it exactly as I show you.
>
> "People from throughout the world will come to receive the best medical science and the best healing prayer. They will come to know: 'I am the Lord that healeth thee.'
>
> "You shall call it the CITY OF FAITH.
>
> "Never permit anything to stand in the way of holding faith in Me and hope to all who come. I want you to cause My love to flow toward all.

"You will pray for the sick all your life. The City of Faith I have commissioned you to build will enlarge and extend your personal healing ministry throughout the world. It will be a seed multiplied in millions of lives who otherwise would never know true healing power that I have provided for them.

"You are a Man of Prayer, an evangelist of My healing for the whole man. You live under My authority and in the power of the Holy Spirit. This is what ties everything together and makes it Mine for you, and Mine for those who follow you to take My healing power to your generation, the generation of man. Have I ever failed you when you trusted Me as your Source? When you put in your seed? When you expected miracles? I told you that you will not build it, I would build it through you. You have never healed anyone or built anything; I have done the healing and the building. I have worked through you as My chosen man. I have also worked through the men and women I have chosen to be your Partners. They are chosen as you are chosen. I have spoken in their hearts and they have put in their seed out of their need and I have multiplied it. Through their Seed-Faith I am meeting their needs. It is through their Seed-Faith I am doing great things for them, and I am building great things through you for the healing of the people. I have been preparing them to launch out in the deep with their giving and receiving."

I cannot begin to convey to you the joy that surged through me when I heard God say that the health-care center was to be called the CITY OF FAITH. I thought my heart would burst. *FAITH!* God was focusing on the very core of the issue...*FAITH!*

My entire life had been built on faith. Everything I had ever attempted had been as an act of my faith, a seed of my faith. Each time we had started a building at Oral Roberts University, our top administrators at both the ministry and the university had gathered to give an offering from their own wallets as a seed of faith...and then we dug a hole in the ground by faith, and began to expect God to multiply our faith and build His building. I knew without a doubt that medicine administered with FAITH could and would do what medicine administered without faith could never do.

God has a newness of life for every person. He rains upon even the driest of deserts and causes life to spring forth. The words of the prophet Isaiah were seared into my mind:

> For as the rain cometh down, and the snow from heaven, and returneth not thither, but watereth the earth, and maketh it bring forth and bud, that it may give seed to the sower, and bread to the eater:
>
> So shall my word be that goeth forth out of my mouth (ISAIAH 55:10–11).

Every word and phrase of that passage took on new life for me, and especially the phrases "seed to the sower" and "bread to the eater." These were words I not only believed to the core of my being, but they were words I had used in my teaching and preaching on a regular basis.

Although I had been teaching the principles of Seed-Faith living to my Partners for nearly a decade at this point, I felt a renewed desire to place greater emphasis on Seed-Faith. The three great and overlapping principles of Seed-Faith are these:

- **God Is Our Source.** God is the Source of every person's total supply.

- **Give as a Seed of Faith.** All types of giving should be planted with faith.

- **Expect a Miracle.** We are to be continually in expectancy
for a harvest of miracles from God.

Seed-Faith is not a 1-2-3 formula. Rather, these three truths of
God are to be fully activated in us at all times. Our giving is to God…
with faith. Our receiving is from God…by faith. The Bible links
giving and receiving in numerous passages. All giving is ultimately
to God, all receiving is ultimately from God. He is our Source!

One of my favorite verses is found in the apostle Paul's writings
to the Galatians: "Be not deceived; God is not mocked: for
whatsoever a man soweth, that shall he also reap. For he that
soweth to his flesh shall of the flesh reap corruption; but he that
soweth to the Spirit shall of the Spirit reap life everlasting. And
let us not be weary in well doing: for in due season we shall reap,
if we faint not. As we have therefore opportunity, let us do good
unto all men, especially unto them who are of the household of
faith" (GALATIANS 6:7–10).

There is a due season for every seed of faith a person plants.

We are to be people who do not just sow a seed of faith on one
occasion, but we are to sow continually. We must not grow weary
or lax in our giving.

We are to look to God at all times for the multiplication of our
seed into a harvest of those things we need most in our life at any
given time.

I have lived by these principles for more than seventy years. I
know they work. I've seen these principles not only in my own life,
but in the lives of tens of thousands of people who have written
to tell me about the miracles they have received from God after
they began trusting Him as their Source of total supply and begin
planting seeds of faith in God's work.

In late 1977 God underscored to me the importance of joining the
delivery systems of medicine and prayer, and also of emphasizing
Seed-Faith as never before:

"All the preachers in the world will never do it. All the physicians in the world will never do it. They are doing good things, but separately. They are not joining the delivery systems of medicine and prayer... they are not healing the whole man.... The Holy Dove can fly only as both its wings are working.

"You have not been bold enough. You have allowed the adversaries to hinder you. You must pay no attention to the adversaries. You must pay total attention to Me.

"Remember, above all things—yes, above all things!—I want My children to prosper, and to be in health, with that prosperity tied to their souls. No Partner you have has ever had enough prosperity because he hasn't learned to receive. He has never had enough health in his total person because he doesn't know how to receive. He has never had enough spiritual power because he doesn't know how to receive. That's because he hasn't understood the miracle of Seed-Faith.

"I've appointed you to share Seed-Faith with your Partners to teach them to look to Me as their Source of total supply, to plant their seeds of faith, then expect to receive. To receive enough prosperity. To receive enough total health. To receive My supply for all their needs. To receive not according to any human measurement but according to the riches of My Son Jesus in heaven."

One of the hallmark verses of my life has been 3 John 2: "Beloved, I wish above all things that thou mayest prosper and be in health, even as thy soul prospereth." The day I discovered that verse in my Bible was a day that changed my life and Evelyn's life. God desires

for His people to receive what they need in *abundance*. And the key is faith.

There in the desert time of our grieving, God breathed new life into me and into my ministry. As part of His message to me, God said:

> "In the new CITY OF FAITH, I want My resources used, medicine, but more than medicine; prayer, but more than prayer. I want the thinking and the atmosphere charged with faith and hope, where My healing love permeates the entire place. I want the people who come for medical care to feel this atmosphere in their minds, in their spirits, for it will open them up to having a great opportunity for a cure. Inspire everyone to have faith and hope in Me as the Source of healing.
>
> "You will pray for the healing of the sick all your life. The City of Faith will enlarge the borders of My healing power throughout the world. The idea will go into all nations as a result of the City of Faith. It will be a seed, which I will multiply to reach millions who have not known before that I AM the Source of their healing and their health, spiritually, mentally, and physically."

God's words to me about the City of Faith gave way to a tremendous series of visions. As clearly as anything I have ever seen with my natural eyes, God filled my Inner Vision with details of the buildings. They were to be towering buildings from a single base—three towers, one 600 feet in height for clinical purposes, one 300 feet in height as a hospital, and one 200 feet in height for research and continuing education. The towers were to be connected on a four-story base. Everything was gold in color, a crown jewel rising upward, pointing toward God.

I had never thought of building a hospital, but during those days in the desert God revealed to me in greater detail than I had ever seen before the importance of having a place of FAITH in which prayer and medicine were to be merged as if two great streams were flowing together into one healing river.

Evelyn, and my son Richard, had dozens of questions. So did I.

We returned home feeling rested and at peace, and I immediately called Jim to share with him the plan God had revealed to me. Jim said, "This could revolutionize the way sick people are cared for."

His words had a prophetic ring. I felt a leaping in my heart and a boldness in my spirit.

We announced a few weeks later that we would be building the City of Faith. Every day after that for more than a decade, I felt as if I was in a wrestling match with Satan. Jesus' statement recorded in JOHN 10:10 took on personal reality for me: "The thief cometh not, but for to steal, and to kill, and to destroy: I am come that they might have life, and that they might have it more abundantly."

I clung to that truth.

What God's Words to Me Mean to Your Life Today

No matter what God has purposed for your life, and no matter where you are today in your accomplishing that purpose, God's words to me in 1977 have meaning for you. What God said to me I have no doubt He desires to say to you, in ways that are totally applicable to your situation.

1. Every method of God functions by FAITH.

You will find that truth from cover to cover in the Bible.

God called a man named Moses to raise his rod and hand over a sea and as Moses acted with *faith*, that sea parted so the children of Israel could walk across it on dry ground.

God called a young man named David to go up against the champion of the Philistines, and as David acted with faith, he ran

toward his enemy and defeated him with one stone hurled from a whirling slingshot.

God called a young woman to bear His child, and as Mary acted with *faith*, she conceived and gave birth to Jesus.

Every method that produces anything good on this earth today has a kernel of FAITH in it that ensures the success of that method.

God may very well speak to you about your faith, calling you to use your faith in new ways—to activate your faith and begin to give in faith, trusting God to multiply your seeds of faith into a tremendous harvest of miracles.

2. God is your Source in all things necessary for an abundant life.

He is the Source of your healing.

He is the Source of your business success.

He is the Source of your ministry.

He is the Source of the provision and protection you need to live daily in this world.

He is the Source of your loving, productive, beneficial relationships.

He is the Source of genuine, life-giving spiritual power in your life.

He is the Source of your total supply of all things necessary for you to have an abundant life.

God wants every person to be reminded—continually—that He is your Source and everything else is an instrument or method in His hand.

3. God has something for you to give, and something for you to receive...at all times.

Giving and receiving are cyclical and continuous. We all must have multiple cycles of giving and receiving in operation at all times. Giving and receiving are not isolated events. They are a continuous, seamless lifestyle linked to faith.

God speaks to every person about what to give and where to plant that seed of your giving. Once a seed is planted, you must persevere in faith until God sends the harvest, knowing that every seed has a "due date" for harvest on God's calendar.

4. God often seeks for us to merge various methods for greater effectiveness and potency.

More and more we are seeing what I call "cluster effects." Two or more medications might work together to produce a result that is far greater than any one medication by itself. Two or more procedures might be melded together for more efficiency in a factory manufacturing or delivery system. Two or more companies might merge for greater impact in the marketplace.

Jesus taught His disciples to gather together for ministry and prayer in groups of "two or more"—and He said He would be in their midst in a way that was more effective than one person's praying alone. He called upon His followers to "agree in prayer," indicating that the agreement of two or more is more potent than one alone standing in faith. (SEE MATTHEW 18:19–20.)

God may have a very specific word for you today about the ways in which He wants various methods in your life to come together in a new way, for a greater impact, efficiency, or potency.

One God-given method rooted in faith is powerful. Two or more God-given methods rooted in faith and *merged together* are more powerful.

We have only begun to see the full harvest that God wants to send to His children on this earth. That harvest is very likely going to be released as believers come together in unity of purpose, merging their methodologies and releasing their faith as one.

Evaluate Your Own Heart

In what areas of your life is God desiring to "rain upon your desert" and cause a newness of life and energy to spring forth?

Are you truly trusting God as your Source?

Are you in a rhythm of continuous giving and receiving? If not, the place to begin is likely with giving.

Are you trusting God to show you new, innovative ways of merging various methods in your life and work for greater impact?

Listen.

And listen again.

Listen today.

God Is Bigger

No matter the size of your problem or need, God is greater.

Ye are of God, little children, and have
overcome them: because greater is he that
is in you, than he that is in the world.

—1 JOHN 4:4

We did not build the City of Faith in isolation. We still had the ongoing operational expense related to our television ministry and ORU, which the Oral Roberts Evangelistic Association was subsidizing every month. We were establishing the professional graduate schools of business, theology, and law, and were recruiting faculty for them. We were establishing the School of Medicine, which meant recruiting faculty and purchasing the very expensive equipment necessary for a top-flight medical training center.

I began to hold the City of Faith project before our Partners, month after month, telling them the cost of each part of the construction. Some months the money rolled in. Other months we ran out of money before we ran out of month! When the money came in, we built; when it didn't, we stopped. Time after time, we would come right up to a payment deadline, and that very day, checks would arrive to cover the cost.

I kept nothing back from my Partners. I have always had a very deep feeling in my heart for the people who have partnered with me for the saving of souls and the deliverance and healing of people. I faithfully prayed over the needs they sent to me, and I continue to do that today.

Checks from many of my Partners usually averaged around $25 a month. As the construction bills and costs related to the School of Medicine and City of Faith increased, some Partners made special pledges over and above their regular monthly giving. In addition, some people we had never heard from before wrote and sent checks, wanting a part of this new approach to joining prayer and medicine. Every dollar counted.

I personally faced a tremendous challenge when it came to juggling my time and energy. I continued with taping television programs, fulfilling my role as president of Oral Roberts University, spending time in the Prayer Tower praying over the needs of our Partners, giving input on the many facets of the new graduate schools and the City of Faith, and all the while, feeling the tremendous pressure related to the finances required.

Soon after we announced the building of the City of Faith, Saul Yager, who by then had retired from legal practice, met with an attorney for Mount Sinai Hospital in New York City. The man was incredulous that one person would undertake the challenge of building such a massive complex, which he calculated would cost $100 million or more. He asked Saul, "Where is all the money coming from?" Saul smiled and said, "He is going to get it from God." Saul, a Jew, believed God owned all the money in the world. As a Christian, I believed the same thing. Even so, God never seemed to send any "extra" money. He always moved upon the hearts of people so we had "just enough."

We opened the School of Medicine in 1978, on schedule. The medical school accreditation team later told us after their evaluation, "You've done your homework." We projected that the City of Faith would be ready for patients and clinical training in 1981. We needed a temporary "residency" agreement with a hospital for our first class of twenty medical students, and we were able to enter into an affiliation agreement with St. John's Hospital in Tulsa. They agreed to handle the residency training for our first class during their third and fourth years of medical school, but they indicated they would be unable to handle the needs once we had taken in our expected full class size of fifty students. There could be no delay in the completion of the City of Faith.

Construction continued. We had a wonderful day of celebration when the three towers were "topped out." They stood as giant unfinished "shells" of buildings, but there they were on the acreage just south of Oral Roberts University!

And then, the money seemed to dry up almost overnight.

Our Partners began to write that they were unable to continue giving beyond their usual monthly amount. Some people assumed that we needed no more funds now that the buildings were at their

full height. There was nothing left over to finish the facility and still maintain operations in all other areas of the ministry. I had no idea where to turn or what to do.

One Sunday evening, I got in my car and drove to the edge of the ORU campus. The sun was starting to go down as I sat and stared at the unfinished buildings before me about a third of a mile south.

All sorts of "what if" thoughts raced through my mind. I'm sure you've had similar thoughts—"What if we can't meet the deadline?", "What if we fail?", "what if...what if...what if." Let me assure you, too many "what if" questions can cause a downward spiral that can lead to significant discouragement.

Then suddenly, I had a vision of Jesus standing behind the unfinished City of Faith buildings. He was only visible to me from the waist up, but His image was at least one and a half times as tall as the tallest tower, which was six hundred feet.

Jesus looked me in the eyes and then leaned over and picked up the City of Faith skyscrapers on their four-story platform as easily as a child might pick up a toy replica of the buildings. And He said to me:

> "See how easy it is for Me to lift it?
>
> "I own all the gold and silver in the earth. It was I who made Abraham rich in faith, in love, in vision, in money, so he would be the father of all who have faith. And because Abraham had faith, I stopped the devil from stealing his money. Neither you nor any of My children are poor except when you fail to know who I am."

A word from God changes everything.

All of the doubts and "what if" questions evaporated in that moment.

The words of Jesus kept ringing in my ears long after His visage vanished from my inner sight.

"See how easy it is for Me to lift it?"

Truly, how EASY it is for Jesus to lift any problem or solve any need!

The Bible tells us that the name of Jesus is higher than the name of anything that might inflict itself upon us or afflict us from within. The apostle Paul wrote to the Philippians: "God also hath highly exalted him [Jesus], and given him a name which is above every name: That at the name of Jesus every knee should bow, of things in heaven, and things in earth, and things under the earth; and that every tongue should confess that Jesus Christ is Lord, to the glory of God the Father" (PHILIPPIANS 2:9–11).

No disease is greater than the name of Jesus.

No financial need is greater than the name of Jesus.

No problem in a person's business or family or church is greater than the name of Jesus.

NOTHING is greater.

Jesus was making it very plain to me that I had become so focused on the enormity of my problem—and trust me, three unfinished skyscrapers are an enormous problem—that I had failed to see that Jesus was still in control, Jesus had all of the finances necessary at His command, and that Jesus was the solution to any challenge that might still lie before us in the completion of the City of Faith.

I could hardly wait to tell my Partners and my associates in the ministry and university about my vision from the Lord and the words of Christ Himself to my heart.

The media, of course, got it wrong. It wasn't the first time the media would err when it came to reporting about Oral Roberts, and it wasn't the last time. The headlines appeared across the nation that I said Jesus was nine hundred feet tall.

They failed to note that I had experienced a vision of Jesus.

They failed to report accurately what Jesus spoke to me in this vision.

And they failed to report accurately that I saw Jesus nine hundred feet tall only *from the waist up!*

Many people laughed at the news report. But, there were also many people who caught the truth of what had happened to me. They began to believe that Jesus was greater than any problem they were facing personally!

Jesus was bigger than their cancer diagnosis, the foreclosure on their home, their loss of a job, their heart disease, the troubles in their marriage or with their children...and on and on. They began to get their eyes off their problems and back on the Source of their healing and deliverance.

And, they began to understand with renewed importance that the City of Faith was not completed and that it needed to be completed to send a message to the world that FAITH in God can move an entire mountain range of problems.

In the final analysis, the vision of Jesus and His words to me were confirmation once again that we must never fail when it comes to focusing our faith and placing all of our trust in God. Our faith does not lie in other people—not in what they say, what they do, or what they give.

The City of Faith opened, on schedule, in 1981.

What God's Words to Me Mean to Your Life Today

The message of God to me about the City of Faith has direct relevance to your life, regardless of who you are or what you are facing today. The messages to you are very simple, yet extremely profound.

1. God is bigger than your biggest need.

You may be feeling overwhelmed by something right now. You may be troubled by fears of terrorism or news of war. You may be exhausted in thinking about a physician's diagnosis or prognosis.

You may be overwhelmed about what to do as you stare at a mountain of bills, or realize that you might lose your home. You may feel panic at the prospect that your spouse might be walking away or your child might be running away or that a loved one might be dying.

God desires to say to you, "Get your eyes off your problem. Get your eyes on Me!"

2. God has all the resources you need in His hands, which are outstretched to you so you might receive those resources by faith.

God has riches you can't begin to fathom. He has unlimited resources, unlimited wisdom, unlimited understanding, unlimited methods, unlimited love.

The biggest problem you are facing is not your lack of something or someone. Your biggest problem is a *failure* to trust God to provide for you.

Renew your faith.

Get your eyes back on the Source of your supply.

There's an old gospel song that says, "Turn your eyes upon Jesus, look full in His wonderful face, and the things of earth will grow strangely dim, in the light of His glory and grace."

All of the comfort you need right now will come to you as you look fully into the wonderful face of Jesus.

Jesus loves you beyond all measure. He has all the resources you need in His hands. His hands are extended to you today for you to receive by faith what He freely gives.

Evaluate Your Own Heart

Are you overwhelmed by a problem or need right now?

Do you truly believe that God is bigger than your biggest need? Bigger than your biggest problem?

Listen.
And listen again.
Listen today.

CHAPTER FOURTEEN

A Matter of Total Obedience

There is only one standard for obedience: a TOTAL YES to whatever God commands.

And it shall come to pass, if thou shalt hearken
diligently unto the voice of the LORD thy God, to
observe and to do all his commandments which
I command thee this day, that the LORD thy
God will set thee on high...

—DEUTERONOMY 28:1

After the City of Faith opened, we faced a series of problems besides the financial ones that had been almost constant during the years of construction. One of the major problems was a lack of patients with a sufficient diversity of diseases to satisfy the American Medical Association requirements for adequate residency programs. We faced further difficulty when we discovered that our efforts to train up "missionary physicians and dentists" did not seem to be succeeding. Some of the students concluded that they were not called to become missionaries after their training was complete, and in many other cases, the students were shackled by enormous loans that left them with contractual obligations to pay off those loans before they could go overseas.

Perhaps the most damaging problem we faced was a tremendous confusion that developed simultaneously on two fronts. I am fully aware that the Bible teaches clearly that confusion is a major tactic of the enemy of our souls. What God does is orderly and straightforward. What the devil does is fragmented and frayed. We were under spiritual attack of the worst kind, for when confusion is the tactic it becomes increasingly difficult for people to sift through a barrage of false information and discern the truth so they might obey it.

Throughout my ministry I had learned and disciplined myself to think in wholes, not parts. The ORU graduate and professional schools, along with the college of arts and sciences, were given a mandate to interrelate. I saw Spirit-filled professors in each school—under the steady and able leadership of ORU's academic provost, Dr. Carl Hamilton—meeting together to harmonize their disciplines and goals so that the students in all disciplines might be prepared in an optimal way to meet needs. I saw students making special efforts to relate their disciplines to other disciplines so they might become whole men and women, and in turn, take a message of wholeness to the world.

All around us, however, were forces that were *not* intent on either wholeness or integration. It became very clear that some in the church world were very opposed to the merging of prayer and medicine. They wanted medicine to be a "last resort" if God failed to heal supernaturally. It became clear that many in the medical world were equally opposed to the merging of prayer and medicine. They wanted prayer to continue to be something that was "tacked onto" medical care, rather than something regarded as an equal healing stream.

As we approached 1986, five years after the City of Faith opened, we had dropped behind several million dollars in carrying on our ministry, the university, and our medical enterprises. I spoke on television about the shortfall and wrote letters about the shortfall to my Partners. They did not respond. I quickly recognized that in addition to feeling confused about how the City of Faith might be an extension of God's healing power to the nations, a significant percentage of the Partners were simply exhausted financially and in all other ways. I understood that. I felt exhausted, too, at the difficulties that seemed to be coming from all directions.

Then, on my sixty-eighth birthday—January 24, 1986—God spoke:

> "You're on the last rung of the ladder and your next move, you will be standing before Me. And you will be telling Me why you have not sent out the healing team missions. You have not done what I told you to do. You have not sent out the healing teams to the ends of the earth. You have not done it and your next move you'll be standing in front of Me telling Me why."

God put a deadline and dollar amount on His mandate in a way that He had never done before in my experiences of hearing His voice:

> "I have told you to turn around My medical school and to raise $8 million to send the young physician graduates to the nations. You have until March 31 to get it done. If you don't, then your work is finished, and I am going to call you home."

At first, I felt glad and somewhat relieved when I heard God say that He might be calling me home. In going to be with the Lord, I saw a shedding of burdens, a laying down of armor, a feeling of finally arriving home, a wonderful eternity of being at rest! I was tired from the years of battling to get the City of Faith built and the School of Medicine established. Going "home" to heaven sounded like a wonderful idea to me. The part that was troublesome was God's saying He would be requiring me to tell Him why I had not done what He had told me to do.

In an instant, it became crystal-clear to me that the real issue from God's perspective was *obedience*.

God sees only two categories of human response to His commands: obedience and disobedience. Plain and simple, if I failed to do what God said, I fell into the category of disobedience. God uses those who are obedient. He does not use those who are disobedient. If I was not useful to God, there was absolutely no reason for me to stay on this earth. My work would be finished.

I don't expect every person to understand that as clearly as I understood it then and continue to understand the role of obedience today. I was raised in a home where obedience to God was paramount. My mother, especially, had drilled into me the vital importance of obedience. I can still close my eyes and hear her say, "Oral, obey God!" Momma didn't care how hard disobedience might be or how much disobedience might cost in terms of reputation or favor. Nothing mattered except obedience to God. There were no justifications and no excuses for a failure to obey.

My experiences during three and a half decades of healing ministry and building for God—including a university and the City of Faith—had confirmed the importance of absolute obedience to me. What God said, I did. There was no life apart from a life of *obedience*.

Not only that, but God was saying in very direct terms that obedience in this matter of sending healing teams was a life-and-death matter. Most of all, the lives of millions of sick people around the world were at stake.

I recalled a time in the life of Moses when God told Moses to return to Pharaoh for the deliverance of the Israelites from Egypt. On the way there, God required that Moses be circumcised and that he circumcise his son. Moses delayed and became deathly ill. Finally, Moses' wife did the circumcisions and Moses recovered. God clearly wanted Moses to understand that obedience was absolutely essential if Moses was going to live to fulfill God's call on his life. (SEE EXODUS 4:24–26.)

I believe obedience was the rock-bottom requirement for all of the major prophets throughout the Bible. Obedience was required of Jesus, and He in turn required obedience from His followers. Three times on the last night He was with His disciples before His crucifixion, Jesus said to His followers, "If you love me, keep my commandments." (SEE JOHN 14.)

The following Sunday I relayed the words God had spoken to my heart on our television program. It was the fastest way I knew to get a message to my Partners—a message that I tried hard to explain in terms of obedience and the importance God places on obedience.

The media picked up on what I said and front-page headlines circled the world overnight: "Oral Roberts Says God Is Going to Kill Him if He Doesn't Raise $8 Million."

The media reported words I never said. Nevertheless, many people chose to believe what they read or heard.

News anchors and talk-show hosts scoffed, comedians made jokes, and even leaders in the church world weighed in with criticism.

There was no mention of obedience.

There was no mention of life-and-death seriousness or commitment.

There was no mention of the reason for raising the $8 million—to send healing teams around the world to merge prayer and medicine.

Even so…in the midst of all the laughter, derision, and confusion, we received $8 million. We used the money to scholarship our medical students and to send our first healing teams overseas with a message of wholeness and the merging of prayer and medicine.

The Closing of the City of Faith

The American Medical Association came annually to evaluate our medical school and our residency programs at the City of Faith. The year came toward the close of the 1980s when we recognized a major and abrupt shift in the favor we had received from the AMA in earlier years. Previous site teams couldn't say enough good things about our program, facilities, and the men who led our medical school and the City of Faith. This year, things were dramatically different. I did not know *why*, but I knew things were changing and the change was beyond my control or power to influence it.

A year prior to this particular site team visit from the AMA, David Wilkerson, a minister who has spent much of his life dealing with drug addicts in New York City, came to Tulsa to speak to the student body of ORU in a chapel service. Afterwards, he asked to speak with me privately. His prophetic words to me went something like this: "Oral, God had you raise up the medical and dental schools and the City of Faith. He wanted prayer and medicine merged, and He wanted your medical and dental graduates to become missionaries as you were advocating. But I have a word from the Lord. You have made the point He wanted made. The world knows it, the church knows it, and you are to close these institutions."

He just about shocked me out of my shoes.

I said, "Are you sure God gave you this prophetic message for me?"

He said, "I am."

I felt as if a knife was ripping through my stomach. David, however, never batted an eye.

I said, "Is there anything else you feel you must tell me?"

He said, "Yes. Don't be concerned about what true Christians or your Partners will think of you. They know and feel your heart and know that you have obeyed God. They will understand. But God is saying to close them down. You've made the point He wanted made."

I didn't really know what to say, so I asked him if he would go with me to tour the City of Faith. He said, "Sure, I'd love to."

We spent two hours going through the City of Faith—with 2.2 million square feet, the City of Faith was the largest medical complex on one base in the world. It took awhile to see all areas of it.

David said, "I feel the presence of God in this place."

I said, "It's been here from day one."

David talked with some of the doctors, nurses, and patients. I asked him to pray for some of the patients so he could see how the Spirit of God was working through prayer and medical care merged together.

David concluded, "This place is different. It is exactly like you have told the world it would be and is."

I said, "But you gave me a prophetic word I was to close all the medical facilities—that God's point has been made."

David didn't answer immediately. He sat down and was quiet for a long time. I sat down beside him and waited. Finally he said, "Oral, my word to close it down still holds. You've done what God wanted you to do. It's over as far as this place is concerned, but *the concept has been released and you can add no more to it.*"

We parted on that note and I neither saw nor heard from David Wilkerson after that.

I did not act immediately on what David had said even though I knew he had spoken with full conviction and compassion that his words were from God.

It took two years of agonizing pain and continued struggle, several confirming words from others including prophetic words that we were to close down the medical school and City of Faith, and many disappointments—but by the end of 1989, we had closed

the School of Dentistry, the School of Medicine, and the City of Faith. (The School of Nursing remains at ORU and is thriving.)

Few people have had their losses reported more widely.

We were not the only ones in the Christian world, of course, who were going through devastatingly difficult times. Countless churches and ministries were reeling—and especially, it seemed, those who were on television. The problems, in part, were related to widely publicized indiscretions and scandals involving some well-known ministers at the time. Even though we had never had sexual or financial scandals in our ministry, we seemed to be painted with a wide brush of criticism and disdain.

There may have been many other reasons or forces about which we did not know. It is difficult to answer "why" questions when you are in the midst of pain and disappointment.

"Do Not Think You Have Failed"

In the years since the closing of the City of Faith, which to me seemed to take away part of my very soul, I have discovered that what *appears* to be a failure is not always a failure.

Everything in life moves forward on ideas. Even though we were unable to stem a rising and eventually overwhelming tide of opposition and misunderstanding and had to close these parts of ORU, it was not before God's idea had been hurled around the world by the media, by the professions, and by the man on the street. Invisibly, an understanding that prayer and medicine belong together, with faith at their root, began to take shape and find means of expression in physicians, hospitals, and other areas of health care around the world.

Because the City of Faith was such a large facility, it captured the attention of the world. And in so doing, the powerful idea of *wholeness* pervading medicine was given a very high profile—

certainly a profile too big to ignore. The phrase "merging medicine and prayer" entered the vocabulary of countless people who had never considered that prayer and medicine were both healing methods of God.

Dr. Harry Jonas, the secretary of the Liaison Committee on Medical Education of the AMA, spoke with me personally when he came to Tulsa to help us relocate our medical students after we announced the closing of the medical school. He said, "Reverend Roberts, do not think you have failed. You have forever changed medicine and the way the medical world looks at it."

I asked, "How could that be, Dr. Jonas?"

He said, "This idea of combining medicine with prayer, with a view toward wholeness, is an idea whose time has come. The idea has reached into virtually every doctor's office, clinic, hospital, nursing school, and nursing practice in the entire world."

I was taken aback. He saw my reaction and said, "I know what it appears like. To be fought as you were, to be misunderstood on such a scale, may have left you thinking everyone in medicine was against you—not so. *The fact is, the idea is bigger than you are.*"

And then he added, "Before you die, you will see that the changes have begun to take place everywhere."

From my perspective, prayer and medicine are a long way from being fully merged, but I do see that changes have *begun* to be made. I have not been in a single doctor's office, clinic, research center, or hospital since the City of Faith closed without finding some who were using prayer in their work and with their patients that was far beyond anything they had done in past decades. Not long ago I saw an advertisement for a hospital that said boldly, "Prayer is part of our health delivery system." I couldn't help but smile.

The truth that prayer and medicine belong together was never more clear to me than in October of 1992. I had a firsthand experience with the merging of God's healing streams.

"It Was God and Us Together"

On October 6, 1992, I suffered a massive heart attack. I have been told that of all the people who are stricken as I was, eighty percent die, another sixteen percent carry dangerous scars on their hearts, and only four percent survive to regain complete health. I was in the four percent.

During the wee hours of the night after I had an angioplasty procedure, I awoke in a dark room and tried to orient myself and recall what had happened. I wanted to pray but I could not get words from my throat. I began to pray silently deep within myself the words that came from the Holy Spirit Himself. A knowing settled over me as God allowed me to interpret the unknown tongue I was praying in my spirit: "You shall live and not die."

Instantly I fell asleep.

I awoke in the morning to hear my son Richard praying in the Spirit, and then as he took me in his arms, he said, "Dad, the Holy Spirit has just told me, 'You shall not die but live.'"

Moments later Dr. John Hagee of the Cornerstone Church of San Antonio, who had flown with Richard on the plane from Dallas, came into my room and not having heard Richard, he said to me, "Brother Oral, God has said this is not unto death. You shall live and not die."

No sooner had he spoken those words than Dr. Tommy Barnett, pastor of the large First Assemblies of God Church in Phoenix, came to my bedside. Without knowing what the Spirit had said or what either Richard or John had spoken to me, Tommy prayed for me and said exactly the same words, "You shall live and not die."

Within a matter of hours, both Bill Swad, a friend who had flown from Columbus, Ohio, as soon as he heard the word of my heart attack on the national news, and the Reverend Ralph Wilkerson, who had been near me all night long at the hospital, told me the same confirming words.

As these five men surrounded me with their prayers and love, and confirmed God's word to me, I felt as if I had my own private "healing team" fully in place! No one was happier about my recovery from this heart attack than my attending physician at the hospital, Dr. Myla. He said to me later, "It was God and us together who did this."

Yes, indeed—that is the key! *God and us together.*

Prayer and medicine belong together. More and more, we will see them merged, with a greater and greater reliance upon faith as the foundation for all healing. I have no doubt about it.

On what do I base my confidence?

A tremendous seed has been planted in the world. God had told me even before we built the City of Faith that it would be a *seed.* I didn't understand His words then nearly as well as I understand them now. Seeds die as part of their growth into fruitful and productive plants. The City of Faith may have died as a health-care center, but the God-given idea of "merging prayer and medicine in faith" continues to grow and multiply.

It is God's desire that we come into a new understanding of all that makes a person *whole.* And, that we begin to use every method available to us as we seek wholeness rooted in faith. What God desires, God *will* bring to pass.

What God's Words to Me Mean to Your Life Today

There are at least three things that I experienced in the establishment and then the closing of the City of Faith that I believe God wants to say to every person who follows Jesus Christ as Lord.

1. God isn't finished with you yet.

There is no justification and no excuse for disobedience. But, God is also the God who gives second chances. God responds to a

Even so...in the midst of all the laughter, derision, and confusion, we received $8 million. We used the money to scholarship our medical students and to send our first healing teams overseas with a message of wholeness and the merging of prayer and medicine.

The Closing of the City of Faith

The American Medical Association came annually to evaluate our medical school and our residency programs at the City of Faith. The year came toward the close of the 1980s when we recognized a major and abrupt shift in the favor we had received from the AMA in earlier years. Previous site teams couldn't say enough good things about our program, facilities, and the men who led our medical school and the City of Faith. This year, things were dramatically different. I did not know *why*, but I knew things were changing and the change was beyond my control or power to influence it.

A year prior to this particular site team visit from the AMA, David Wilkerson, a minister who has spent much of his life dealing with drug addicts in New York City, came to Tulsa to speak to the student body of ORU in a chapel service. Afterwards, he asked to speak with me privately. His prophetic words to me went something like this: "Oral, God had you raise up the medical and dental schools and the City of Faith. He wanted prayer and medicine merged, and He wanted your medical and dental graduates to become missionaries as you were advocating. But I have a word from the Lord. You have made the point He wanted made. The world knows it, the church knows it, and you are to close these institutions."

He just about shocked me out of my shoes.

I said, "Are you sure God gave you this prophetic message for me?"

He said, "I am."

I felt as if a knife was ripping through my stomach. David, however, never batted an eye.

I said, "Is there anything else you feel you must tell me?"

He said, "Yes. Don't be concerned about what true Christians or your Partners will think of you. They know and feel your heart and know that you have obeyed God. They will understand. But God is saying to close them down. You've made the point He wanted made."

I didn't really know what to say, so I asked him if he would go with me to tour the City of Faith. He said, "Sure, I'd love to."

We spent two hours going through the City of Faith—with 2.2 million square feet, the City of Faith was the largest medical complex on one base in the world. It took awhile to see all areas of it.

David said, "I feel the presence of God in this place."

I said, "It's been here from day one."

David talked with some of the doctors, nurses, and patients. I asked him to pray for some of the patients so he could see how the Spirit of God was working through prayer and medical care merged together.

David concluded, "This place is different. It is exactly like you have told the world it would be and is."

I said, "But you gave me a prophetic word I was to close all the medical facilities—that God's point has been made."

David didn't answer immediately. He sat down and was quiet for a long time. I sat down beside him and waited. Finally he said, "Oral, my word to close it down still holds. You've done what God wanted you to do. It's over as far as this place is concerned, but *the concept has been released and you can add no more to it.*"

We parted on that note and I neither saw nor heard from David Wilkerson after that.

I did not act immediately on what David had said even though I knew he had spoken with full conviction and compassion that his words were from God.

It took two years of agonizing pain and continued struggle, several confirming words from others including prophetic words that we were to close down the medical school and City of Faith, and many disappointments—but by the end of 1989, we had closed

repentant heart and a humble heart. He forgives. He provides a way for people to move forward past their mistakes and failures. We must never think we are beyond being useful to God.

If you feel that you have been disobedient in the past, confess your disobedience to God, ask for His forgiveness, and then receive His forgiveness and begin to move forward to do what you know God has commissioned you to do.

2. Do not call anything a failure.

The truth is, you don't know whether something is a failure or not! Only God can look down the line to see what might become of the seeds you have planted in obedience and faith.

The City of Faith towers are still standing in Tulsa, Oklahoma. The property is presently part of the endowment investments of Oral Roberts University. The potential for that facility is this: If all of the space in that massive complex is leased at a fair-market price, the income could not only supply financial stability for ORU as it continues to grow and develop, but the income could provide ongoing support for *whole-person healing teams* to go around the world with the gospel and the healing power of Christ Jesus. Some of those healing teams would likely be teams of ORU students going out on short-term missions to nations around the world. Some of the healing teams would likely be teams of ORU alumni—from many walks of life, including medicine and dentistry—who would join their efforts in an interrelated way to go into the places around this world where God's light is seen dim, His voice is heard small, and His power is not known. Teams such as these have already gone, and I can see in my spirit countless teams going in the future.

Only God knows the ending of this story from the beginning. I am thoroughly convinced that God is one hundred percent committed to seeing prayer and medicine fully merged, and that whole-person healing founded on faith will become the healing protocol of the future.

If you have failed or made mistakes, give your failure to God. Trust Him to turn *all things* for your good. In truth, God uses everything we do in obedience and faith to bring glory to Himself.

3. Seek to merge prayer and medicine in your own life.

When you are sick, seek the best medicine can offer. At the same time, call for prayer.

In every area of your life, look for ways in which to combine the natural and the supernatural. That is God's desire for you! Listen for Him to speak to you about innovative ways in which to pursue greater wholeness in your personal life and in the lives of those who are in your family, circle of friends, workplace, and church.

God does not separate the material world from the spiritual world. He created them both and designed them to be fully interrelated and integrated.

Ask God to show you how to trust Him for His results in your life as you merge *all* of His healing resources to impact your spirit, soul, and body.

Evaluate Your Own Heart

Are you living in full obedience to God?

Are you discouraged that something hasn't turned out the way you had hoped?

Are you trusting God to merge all of His healing resources on your behalf?

Are you doing your utmost to integrate God's natural world and God's supernatural world?

Listen.

And listen again.

Listen today.

God's Ongoing Word

Changes are coming.
Keep your thoughts on Jesus.

[Jesus said,] Lo, I am with you always, even
unto the end of the world.
—MATTHEW 28:20

everal years ago I was in a restaurant of the hotel where I was staying in Atlanta, Georgia, and God began to speak to me in a way that I knew I needed to record for future reference. I immediately began to write as He spoke in my spirit. His words flowed like a waterfall, sentence after sentence, cascading into my spirit so that I could scarcely keep up in writing down what He said.

As I read back over what God had spoken, I determined that much of His message was primarily for me personally—for Oral Roberts, a follower of Christ Jesus who had completed the most active years of his ministry. I felt great encouragement, but I did not see a reason to share these words with my Partners, associates, or even some members of my family.

The more I have read these words in recent days, however, the more I have come to see that these words might also be for you. What God has said to me He desires to say to any man or woman who seeks to follow Him and fulfill His purposes on this earth.

This, I believe, is God's ongoing word to me. I trust Him to speak to you directly about what you are to gain from this message and how you are to respond to it.

As I have said repeatedly:

Listen.

And listen again.

Listen now.

> "You are going to walk on the mountaintops and the valleys. There will be no difference between them for you from now on, for I am giving you the sight of Abraham, far-seeing sight. In your old years you will give many prophecies and not a one will fall to the ground. Not a one will be unanswered. I will give you thousands of sons and daughters, even tens of thousands, who will have your level of My Spirit and your level of faith and sight.

"You are like Noah in your lifestyle. Noah walked among the people. He talked like them. He dressed like them but he did not have their spirit in any way. He was totally unmistakably unlike them in his spirit. That's how he found favor in My sight. And because he was righteous and moved only by faith among all those who were completely evil, I spoke to him and he heard every word plainly. He took My commands with his whole being. And he became the man, with his partner family, through whom I changed the course of all mankind and produced a new people. Among them were Abraham who saw the entire future and knew I would prevail upon the earth. You have Abraham's far-reaching sight for this generation. Only it is with My healing power for everything you touch and everything you attempt.

"No demons shall conquer you. Satan himself will not destroy you. I own you, and I touch you when I will. Because I know you have obeyed Me completely all these years, I hold you in My hand at all times.

"Keep your thoughts on Jesus. He knows what this next prophetic move is and what will be life-changing for God's people.

"The wealth of the sinners is about to be released and placed in the hands of the just, which is one of the greatest signs of the last days. Your sons and daughters in the Lord will rise up and call you blessed, but only for a flash of a second, for they will see you transparent and will look right through you and see Me. And I will give them the level of your faith.

"Great and mighty changes are coming through faith that will more than match the great and mighty technological changes that are coming—and the loud

and injurious changes being brought about by many, many humanists who are so alienated from Me they cannot see their hands in front of them. The ditches dug deep are awaiting them and their tune will change to loud cries of despair, but they will no more change than the world changed in Noah's day.

"Standing like tall sentinels shining My light into their darkness will be changes I have wrought through your hearing and obeying Me, no matter the cost to you personally or to your family. I have received glory from your acuteness in hearing My voice and your simple obedience to do all I have told you. I will share My love with you in measures you have known only when you have been anointed, and have it continually as a force inside you that will not subside. Many will feel that love unexpectedly and be instantly changed by it and will see their future rising, their spirit surging, their faith leaping.

"A mighty and continuous release of the wealth of the sinner heaped up for the last days will astound them at first as they fail to understand it is a sign of the end times that they can stand on like solid rock. As My people received the release of the wealth of the Egyptians, but none of their diseases, so they could make the long, hazardous journey through the uncharted wild wilderness to reach the Promised Land, so the flow of the wealth of the sinners they've heaped up from My people these last days will help them get through the morass of unbelieving man. They will see far beyond the darkness of persecutions into the sunlight of faith. The flow of the wealth of the sinners into the hands of My servants will reveal to them that the earth and its fullness is Mine and all

I have is theirs. They've not really known this before. This will change the status quo in what men call My church.

"You have never believed you were special and that is good. You have believed any specialness you have comes only through My anointing on you. I have enabled you to build your life pattern on that, but now it will slowly and carefully be transferred to tens of thousands of those I am now making leaders and warriors. All the changes I brought about through you to take My healing power to your generation will multiply beyond anything you can imagine. For I am the God that goes beyond all imagination, all dreams and visions, and all that has been perverted by the devil. I am the God of Light. And that light will make the darkness quickly come to an end and be no more. You were born to help make this happen.

"I have been able to trust you and I will trust you the rest of your days. No one will take you out of My hand. Minister to My people and let them minister before the Lord."

May it be so.
Even now, Lord, may it be so.

Using this study guide

This study guide may be used by you personally as you read THE ULTIMATE VOICE. Or, it may be used as you and a friend read and have conversations about the key points in THE ULTIMATE VOICE. Or, it may be used by a small group to generate discussion. In any case, I encourage you to do the following:

1. Approach your study time in prayer. Ask God to speak to you through THE ULTIMATE VOICE about how He wants to lead you into deeper spiritual principles. Ask the Lord to quicken in you a renewed vision of His plan and purpose for your life, as well as the lives of your family members or others in your small group.

2. As you choose someone with whom to discuss this book—or as you are putting together a small group for discussion—choose those who believe that God exists, that God works in and through individual lives today, and that God still speaks in a still small voice directly to individual hearts that are open to Him.

3. THE ULTIMATE VOICE has many biblical references. These are listed in the study guide. I encourage you to read each of those passages of the Bible and allow God's Word to speak directly to you or to others in your group.

4. Close your personal study time—or any conversation or group discussion—with prayer. Ask God to seal to your heart and mind those concepts that He intends for your eternal blessing. Take time to listen to what God may say to you, individually or collectively.

Approach this study with FAITH, believing fully that God has something wonderful to say to YOU!

Contents

CHAPTER ONE

Does God Speak to Every Person?

1. Do you believe God speaks to individual people in today's world? Why?

2. What kinds of evidence do you seek out to confirm that God has spoken to you, or to someone else?

Read these passages of the Bible: Revelation 3:20; Genesis 4:2–16; Genesis 6:13—9:17; Genesis 12:1–2; Genesis 26; Genesis 35; John 9; John 10:3–5; John 18:37; John 14:16–17; John 16:12–13; Acts 9:4–5; Acts 9:11–12; John 14:10–11; Isaiah 55:9–11.

What do these passages say to you about hearing God's voice?

CHAPTER TWO

Why Doesn't Every Person Hear God's Voice?

1. Is there anything in your life that you may need to remove before you can hear God's voice clearly? How will you go about removing that obstacle to your spiritual hearing?

2. Do you believe you are qualified to hear from God? If so, on what basis? If not, why not?

3. Do you really WANT to hear from God?

Read these passages of the Bible: Matthew 11:15; Genesis 3:9–10; 1 John 1:9; Ezekiel 12:2; Matthew 7:11; Hebrews 11:6; Romans 12:3; 2 Chronicles 20:12–13; 1 Samuel 3:9.

What do these passages say to you about your ability or qualifications to hear God's voice?

CHAPTER THREE

God Is the Supreme Communicator

1. Respond to this statement: "God's principles do not change; God's methods do." In what ways do you see evidence of this in the Bible? In what ways have you seen evidence of this in your own life?

2. What methods does God seem to use the most in speaking directly to YOUR spirit?

3. What does it mean to you to have spiritual ears to hear God?

Read these passages of the Bible: Numbers 12:6; Romans 8:28; 1 Kings 18 and 19.

What do these passages say to you about the nature of God, His unchanging truth, and His limitless methods and applications

CHAPTER FOUR

The Nature of God's Messages

1. Respond to this statement: "The messages of God to us are as individualized and unique as we are. They are also as eternal and absolute as God is."

2. How would you describe to another person your relationship with God? To which character traits of God do you respond the most?

3. How has God spoken to YOU about your unique gifts, talents, and purpose in life?

Read these passages of the Bible: Matthew 17:5; Acts 10:34; John 16:13; 1 John 3:1–2; Exodus 3:13–14; Galatians 5:22–23; Romans 12:1–8; 1 Corinthians 12; 1 John 4:1–3; Matthew 7:7; Deuteronomy 18:16, 19:15; 2 Corinthians 13:1.

What do these passages of the Bible say about the messages God desires to speak to you?

CHAPTER FIVE

More than Ready to Hear

1. Have you accepted Jesus Christ as your Savior? Are you seeking to follow Him as your Lord?

2. About what issue or problem, or in what specific way, would you LIKE to hear from God?

Read this verse in the Bible: Psalm 10:17.

What does this verse in the Bible say about the importance of knowing what you desire from God, and then trusting God to prepare your heart to hear His voice?

CHAPTER SIX

God's First Words to Me

1. Do you have an assurance that you truly are a SON or DAUGHTER to God the Father?

2. What do you believe God desires to heal in your life to make you "whole" in spirit, soul (mind and emotions), and body?

3. Do you see a connection between what God has healed, restored, or done in your life AND the greater purpose of your life as a witness for Christ Jesus? In what ways are we ESPECIALLY qualified to minister to others in the area of our own healing?

Read this verse in the Bible: Psalm 85:8.

What does this verse in the Bible say about what God desires to DO in you and through you?

CHAPTER SEVEN

Be Like Jesus

1. Are you seeking to be like other people, or are you seeking to be like Jesus? In what ways do you struggle with peer pressure or pressure from the culture in which you live?

2. What does it mean to you to "be like Jesus"?

Read these passages of the Bible: Mark 1:14, 39; Mark 4:1–2; Mark 6:56; Matthew 28:18–20; Mark 16:15–18.

What does this verse in the Bible say about the importance of knowing what you desire from God, and then trusting God to prepare your heart to hear His voice?

CHAPTER EIGHT

God's Method for Your Effectiveness

1. Have you ever fasted and prayed to receive specific direction from God? If so, what happened?

2. In what ways is God challenging you to be a more EFFECTIVE Christian?

3. Are you willing to obey God "no matter what"?

4. Are you faithful in your walk with the Lord?

5. How much do you want more of God's presence and power?

Read these passages of the Bible: Jeremiah 18:6; 2 Corinthians 12:9; Judges 6 and 7.

What do these passages of the Bible say about the ways in which God requires total obedience to His specific commands? What do they say about the ways in which God empowers a person to fulfill what God commands?

CHAPTER NINE
Urgency and Increase

1. Do you feel urgency in your spirit to influence people to turn to Christ Jesus?

2. In what areas of your life do you feel a need to trust God more?

3. Are you willing to move into areas and take on goals that seem almost impossible in the natural, trusting God to help you fulfill anything He calls you to d o?

Read these passages of the Bible: Joshua 1:1–9; Mark 9:17–27.

What do these passages of the Bible say about God's desire to expand your thinking, expand your efforts, or enlarge your sphere of influence?

CHAPTER TEN
The Fullness of God's Call

1. As you reflect back over the years of your life, in what ways can you see that God has been working on your behalf all the time? In what ways has God positioned you for what might still lie ahead in your life?

2. What does it mean to you to do something "by faith"?

3. Do you have fears or doubts that are keeping you from stepping out by faith or obeying God's call on your life?

Read these passages of the Bible: Hebrews 12:2; Job 26:7; Hebrews 11:3; Esther 4:13–16; Proverbs 3:5–6.

What do these passages of the Bible say about the need for faith as the foundation for your obedience to God?

CHAPTER ELEVEN
No Limits!

1. Are there still people God wants YOU to reach with the gospel? To whom may God be sending you with a message of His love, and His healing and delivering power?

2. Is it time for you to shift to a new method?

3. Are you expecting miracles from God every day, in every area of your life?

Read these verses of the Bible: Psalm 138:8; Matthew 17:20.

What do these verses of the Bible say about God's unlimited power?

CHAPTER TWELVE
Merging Methods in Faith

1. Respond to this statement: "Every method of God functions by FAITH."

2. Are you trusting God to be the SOURCE of all things necessary for an ABUNDANT life?

3. What is it that you believe God wants you to give? To receive?

Read these passages of the Bible: Matthew 9:12; Isaiah 35:1; Isaiah 55:10–11; Galatians 6:7–10; 3 John 2.

What do these passages of the Bible say about God creating something NEW through your life, work, and ministry?

CHAPTER THIRTEEN

God Is Bigger

1. Respond to this statement: "God is bigger than your biggest need."

2. Do you really believe God is more powerful than your strongest enemy, wealthier than your biggest financial need, and wiser than your greatest question or problem? In what ways do you sense the Holy Spirit is challenging you to trust God in a deeper, fuller, richer way?

Read these passages of the Bible: 1 John 4:4; Philippians 2:9–11.

What do these passages of the Bible say about God's infinite ability to work in and through human beings?

CHAPTER FOURTEEN

A Matter of Total Obedience

1. Do you believe, or do others believe, that you have failed in some way? In what ways are you trusting God to use that experience for his purposes?

2. Do you believe you are living in full obedience to God? If not, what are you feeling challenged to do?

3. Are you doing your utmost to integrate God's natural world and God's supernatural world?

Read these passages of the Bible: Deuteronomy 28:1; Exodus 4:24–26; John 14; Romans 8:28.

What do these passages of the Bible say about God's requirement of obedience, and His promise to work all things together for good in the lives of those who are obedient?

CHAPTER FIFTEEN

God's Ongoing Word

1. What do God's words to me in the final chapter of THE ULTIMATE VOICE mean to you...to your family...to your church...to your community?

2. In what ways might God be leading you to stand like a "tall sentinel" shining His light into the darkness of this world?

Read this verse in the Bible: Matthew 28:20.

What does this verse mean to you personally?

Oral Roberts

Oral Roberts has been one of the giants of the Christian faith for more than seven decades. His ministry has spanned the globe with a message of healing and miracles that has reached more than a billion people. He founded Oral Roberts University in Tulsa, Oklahoma—a fully accredited liberal arts university offering more than eighty undergraduate and graduate degree programs. He has written more than 100 books and created the first oral commentary on the New Testament.

Roberts is considered the leading healing evangelist of the twentieth century, a pioneer in Christian television, and without a doubt, one of the nation's most innovative, and at times, controversial communicators. He and his late wife, Evelyn, had four children: Rebecca and Ronald (who now live in heaven), and Richard and Roberta (who live in Tulsa, Oklahoma).